PAPER JEWELRY

OVER **35** BEAUTIFUL STEP-BY-STEP

JEWELRY PROJECTS MADE FROM PAPER

DENISE BROWN

CICO BOOKS

LONDON NEW YORK

Published in 2012 by CICO Books
An imprint of Ryland Peters & Small
519 Broadway, 5th Floor, New York NY 10012
20–21 Jockey's Fields, London WC1R 4BW
www.cicobooks.com

10 9 8 7 6 5 4 3 2 1

A CIP catalog record for this book is available from the Library
of Congress and the British Library.

ISBN: 978-1-908170-96-5

Printed in China

Editor: Miriam Catley
Designer: Louise Leffler
Photographer: Gavin Kingcome and Martin Norris
Stylist: Luis Peral-Aranda
Illustrator: Stephen Dew

PAPER
JEWELRY

ROTATION
PLAN

CONTENTS

INTRODUCTION

This book is for all those people who have ever kept a small scrap of pretty gift wrap because they couldn't bear to throw it away. Now they can reinvent it into something they can actually wear.

The recycling possibilities of paper jewelry are endless; broken bits of chain and odds and ends of old dusty eye shadows and unwanted nail polishes, newspapers, envelopes, junk mail, used gift wrap, foil, and candy wrappers can all be transformed into some fabulous creations. Paper fashions change with the seasons as much as clothes do so my advice is to store all the gorgeous bits of gift wrap that come your way. Don't forget how simply stunning pure white can be and you can reuse as many envelopes as you get delivered. The blue and white interiors make fabulous beads, too.

Handle your jewelry with respect and it will last a lot longer. Never forget your projects are made out of paper. Remember to take your rings and bracelets off when washing your hands and don't go out in the rain when wearing any. Varnishing will harden and protect some of your pieces but the more architectural ones need to be treated with care. I do try and spray them with hairspray, one without lanolin or essential oils, or fixative, to try and harden them as much as possible, but would always advise you to test a small sample first before you spray the whole piece. Some pieces made of papier mâché pulp or quilled or rolled paper can be quite robust but others are more fragile. Think how and when you will wear your piece. If you make a large ring, then wear it on a middle finger so it is protected as much as possible. If you choose to make pompoms or bobbles for a necklace, then don't cover them with a heavy garment.

It's impossible to know all the dyes and components that make up different papers. If you are worried you might be allergic to anything, wear latex gloves. The dye comes out of tissue paper so I always wear gloves when working with that. And, even when varnished, test for color fastness if wearing a brooch or necklace, say, against a pale top.

I've designed projects to suit all skill levels but, even if you consider yourself an expert, make a few extra beads for each project in case of accidents. Or you may want to change your design at the last moment and you'll be grateful for a few spares. In fact, it's hard to give exact measurements and weights as paper weights differ between manufacturers and, when dealing with pulp, no two recipes will be exactly the same. It's the same with thread. If your project is large, then trying to make it with a continuous piece of thread will be cumbersome and you will spend forever trying to keep knots out of it. Use manageable lengths and join them together at appropriate points. For instance, it'll always look better and be easier if you tie a knot so its ends can be hidden inside a large bead. I don't expect you to go out and spend a lot of money on special equipment either. Sometimes, it will come in useful, like a punch, if accuracy is essential, or a quilling tool but you can mostly get by with very little. There are no hard and fast rules to making my projects—only that you have fun!

GENERAL EQUIPMENT

I use very little special equipment but there are some things I can't manage without. I have to have a cutting mat, set square, metal ruler, and craft knife. If I am working on a very precise project, I sometimes buy a shape punch too as it not only makes the shapes more accurate but it also really speeds up the time needed to cut things out. Papier mâché pulp will need a sieve and a blender that you don't mind ruining. And, although you can make holes with a needle while the pulp is wet, I tend to use a simple drill when they are dry.

"SPACER" BEADS

I use a variety of beads to help make projects look more finished. Large papier mâché beads in particular do not sit very well together and a "spacer" bead can really help set them off and improve how they fall. I tend to use seed beads. I often buy bags of mixed sizes and colors. It's impossible to make paper beads to exactly the same shape and size every time, so I like the variation in size and shape that you get from the mixed beads. And, of course, I recycle any old or broken necklace beads I find.

PAPERS

I try everything and you can tell immediately if a paper will work or not. Different techniques do work better with slightly different paper weights but it's always worth a bit of experimentation. Different designs and gift wrap change faster than the seasons so you can mix and match anything you have available for a lot of the projects as they don't rely on you being able to find the exact paper I used. Don't forget to try old maps and newspapers and any old catalogs you have lying around. It's a shame to waste them. Quilling paper comes in such gorgeous colors that I find them irresistible.

GLUE

I use white (PVA) glue all the time but it's always a good idea to test it first when you use it to attach brooch and earring findings, as adhesiveness depends on the surfaces

Old, broken necklaces can be put to good use. These larger gold and pearl beads are excellent to use as the center beads in some projects. The smaller seed beads fit snugly up to irregular paper beads and will make projects look more finished.

Patterned and plain, textured and smooth, thick and flimsy; keep all your scraps of paper as you never know when you might want to experiment with something.

involved and you don't want your gorgeous new project to fall off its backing. Double check it's secure before wearing. I often apply glue with a toothpick but there is a useful fine tip glue applicator that is particularly helpful when quilling.

VARNISHES
I use varnish with different finishes as much as I can as it seals and strengthens the projects. Unfortunately, I just can't varnish them all. In those cases, I use fixative or a basic hairspray without oil or lanolin in the hope that that will protect them a little.

COLOR
Don't forget you are painting onto paper which will turn to a mush if too much water is applied! I do use acrylic and water-based paints, but very carefully. So many papers don't need any color at all as they have a pattern already and they only need a varnish.

FINDINGS
If you have any previous experience in jewelry making, then you may want to make your own. I tend to buy mine from bead shops.

TUBES
For rolling beads, I use small tubes—knitting needles, toothpicks (cocktail sticks), straws—use whatever takes your fancy. Bead shapes will change according to the hole diameter so try out some samples first.

THREAD
I use five main types of thread for stringing beads. Magic thread is a rubbery, clear, elastic thread. This is very good for bracelets that you just want to pull on over your hand. I use thin elastic thread, which is finer than Magic, when I have delicate beads made from tissue paper. It's also good for beads where you want them to move a lot, as in clusters. The nylon thread I use is a clear non-elastic thread and that's particularly useful for beads that need to stay in place more or come out of something at an angle. Beading thread is very fine and can be used either with a special needle or just an ordinary one. It comes in lots of different colors so you can match it to your beads. This is good for clusters of beads that you want to hang naturally, too. Finally, there's cotton thread which you may want to use as you try out a few projects to experiment with.

STYROFOAM
I use a piece of Styrofoam for holding toothpicks (cocktail sticks) with beads attached while glue, varnish, or paint dries.

Brooch and earring findings are easy to buy online or from bead stores, but you could always recycle some from broken earrings you already own.

Ribbons and cords can transform a pedestrian piece into something much more interesting. Make this type of threading material into a feature and let it become part of your design by tying spacing knots or bows between your beads.

✻ ✻ ✻ ✻ ✻ ✻ ✻ ✻ ✻ ✻ ✻ ✻ ✻ ✻ ✻ ✻ ✻

CHAPTER ONE

ROLLING

TECHNIQUES AND EQUIPMENT

The Rolling technique involves rolling long paper triangles into beads. It is a similar technique to Quilling (see pages 70–73) but all the shapes need to be cut out carefully using a craft knife and cutting mat. Other than that, there is no need for any special equipment. I've made some examples using different shaped triangles for you to see different effects (see right).

You can try this technique with all kinds of papers but some are more suitable than others and you'll learn by trial and error what material you prefer. Try using plain paper as well as patterned paper. You can even use old letters as the word fragments can make wonderful patterns.

When threading rolled paper beads be very careful not to pull the thread too tight or it will cut into the paper. These beads finish off neatly but you can trim them down before varnishing to make them even more consistent. As with other types of paper beads, these look great when paired with seed beads to help them sit better together.

ROLLERS

You can use any tube that has a consistent diameter. I often use a wooden toothpick but I make sure to roll up my bead away from the pointed ends. You can use a knitting needle but it's best to use a double-ended one so you can roll it on a work surface if you need to. Whatever you use, don't roll your bead too far away from the end of the roller as it makes the bead more difficult to remove.

DIFFERENT TYPES OF TRIANGLES

There are three factors that will affect the size and shape of the paper beads you make: the thickness and weight of the paper; the dimensions of the paper triangle; and the diameter of the rolling implement.

The thicker the paper, the more ridges a bead will have, and the more irregular it might look. Very thin paper, such as tissue paper, will never make a fat, round bead. A slim triangle will make a bead look fatter than a wide triangle. Also, a very long triangle will make a much rounder looking bead. When a bead is rolled using a wide diameter rolling implement, the ends will be slightly jagged but they can be trimmed off. Bear in mind that the same shape triangle rolled around a toothpick will be much more robust than one done using a large tube as the paper will have gone around the toothpick many more times.

As with a cookery recipe, do not swap between different units of measurement when making the projects, because the conversions are not exact.

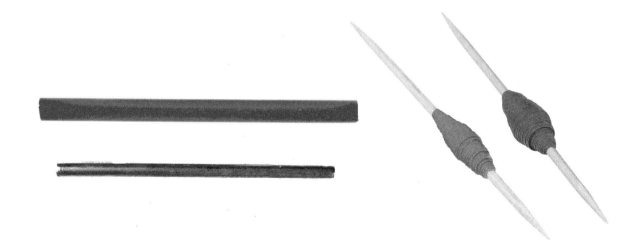

ISOSCELES TRIANGLES

Mostly, I use isosceles triangles (two long sides are of equal length and taper to a central point opposite the shortest side). It is easy to cut a sheet of paper into these shapes.

1 Decide on the length and width of your triangles. For this example, use 4in (100mm) long by 1in (25mm) wide tapering to 0in (0mm).
2 Cut a piece of paper into the 4in (100mm) length and make sure the sides are square.
3 Start along the top width of the paper in the left-hand corner and make a mark at every 1in (25mm) across the whole width. Go to the bottom of the paper and, starting from the corner, make one mark at ½in (12.5mm), and then every 1in (25mm) across the whole width. The first mark on the bottom of the paper must be exactly half the width of the marks along the top.
4 Draw a line from the top left-hand corner down to the ½in (12.5mm) mark at the bottom. This triangle will be discarded as its point is not centered. Draw a line from the ½in (12.5mm) mark up to the first, top, 1in (25mm) mark. This is your first isosceles triangle. Continue to make top to bottom and alternating lines to complete your triangles.

Here are some examples using tissue paper and thin construction paper with three different rolling tools.

Thin tissue paper works best when rolled around something small in diameter. Even a small triangle will make a sturdy bead. When rolled around larger diameter tubes, the beads are more fragile.

Longer triangles of tissue paper will make beads stronger and they can be quite wide. You can see that the edges of the largest bead are irregular and those would need to be trimmed off. The larger beads are still rather delicate.

Construction paper is flexible enough to roll well and substantial enough to use on large tubes.

The longer the triangles, the rounder the beads will be. As some paper sheets are not very long, you can create triangles from two sheets of paper butted together. Roll the first shape as usual, add a dab of glue, and then add the second triangle to complete the bead.

These shapes are similar to the green beads but the longer and wider triangles scale the beads up in size.

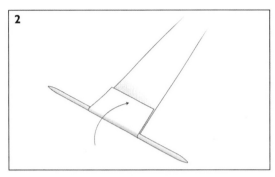

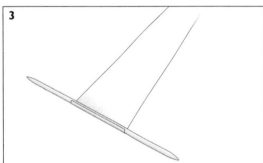

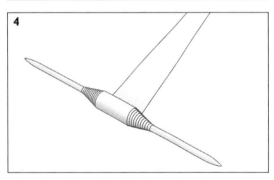

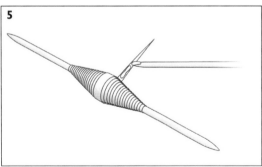

ROLLING TECHNIQUE

Try rolling a bead flat on your work table and then in your hands to see which works best for you.

YOU WILL NEED

Paper triangle (see templates on page 119)

Toothpick or roller of your choice

White (PVA) glue

Styrofoam

1 Place the fattest part of your triangle toward you, with the side you want to see on your bead face down.

2 Put the toothpick horizontally about ¾in (20mm) away from the fattest end and gently fold the end over it. Ensure that the paper is centered on the toothpick.

3 Use your thumbs and gently roll the toothpick back toward you, bringing the paper with it, until only a fraction of the paper is still on the roller.

4 Switch direction and roll the toothpick and paper away from you, keeping the paper tight on the toothpick, and the tip as centered as possible. Sometimes, you can slide the paper into a better position if needed.

5 Continue to roll until ⅜in (10mm) from the tip. Smear a little glue using a toothpick on the remaining triangle and finish off rolling it up. Roll the bead between your thumb and forefinger to press the end down properly.

6 Push the toothpick into some Styrofoam and let the glue dry.

7 Slide the bead off the roller, being careful not to change the shape.

VARNISHING

Varnishing helps to strengthen delicate papers. Clear varnish, whether gloss, matt, or satin, can intensify the colors of beads.

1 Place a bead on the tip of a toothpick and hold its bottom onto the stick with your thumb and forefinger.

2 Paint the top horizontally with the grain of the paper as it will cover any ridges better.

3 Stick the toothpick into some Styrofoam and let it dry.

4 Turn the bead upside down and paint the other half.

PAINTING

Painting can bring an otherwise dull paper bead to life.

Follow Varnishing steps 1–4 (see previous page). You may need more than one coat of paint to give complete coverage.

Always remember to paint with the grain of the paper to ensure you cover the paper completely.

Allow the paint or polish to dry completely before applying a second coat or working with the bead.

Avoid getting paint on the toothpick as this may cause the bead to stick.

Nail polish on white paper gives some amazing effects and you don't need to use varnish on top of it.

PATTERNED PAPER

You can use all sorts of paper to make pretty beads, as shown here. For further examples, see page 26.

USEFUL TIPS

✳ If you use a thicker paper, your bead will show more ridges and it will be fatter than if you used a thinner paper of the same shape.
✳ Different shapes of triangle give different shapes of beads.
✳ Always try one or two beads first as an experiment.
✳ The thickness of the tube that you roll the paper around will affect the shape of the bead.
✳ Paper that is printed with color, such as a color photocopy or a colored paper that is white on the back, may give a white edge all over the bead along the cut edges.
✳ Tissue paper will go darker when you varnish it. The beads will always be delicate so you must not pull the thread too tightly when stringing beads together.
✳ Decide on the thread you will use when considering what to roll your paper around as you may need to pull the thread through some holes more than once.

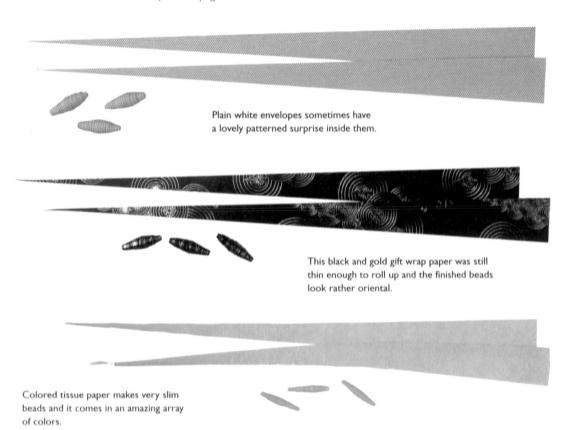

Plain white envelopes sometimes have a lovely patterned surprise inside them.

This black and gold gift wrap paper was still thin enough to roll up and the finished beads look rather oriental.

Colored tissue paper makes very slim beads and it comes in an amazing array of colors.

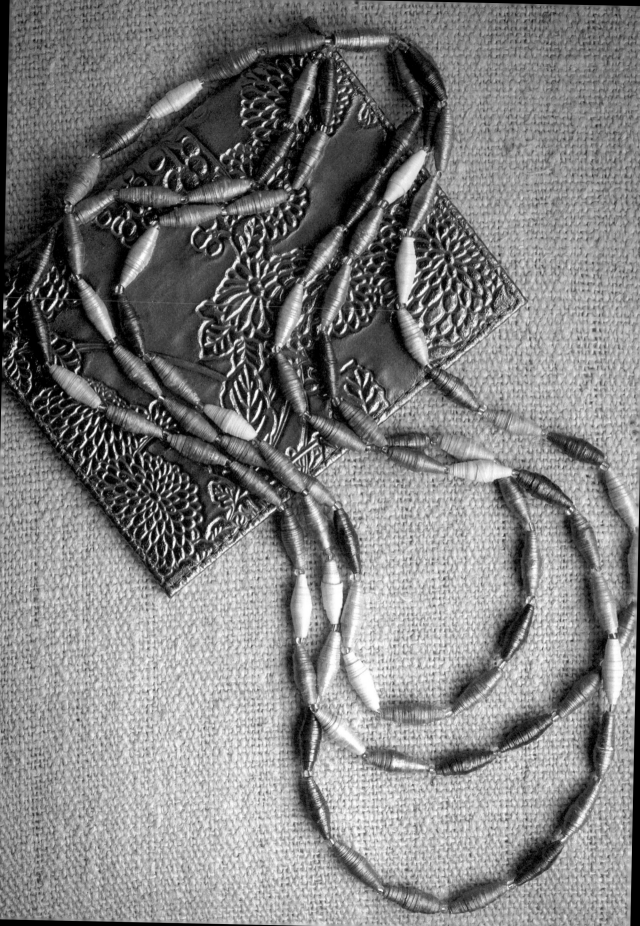

SEED PEARL NECKLACE

Delicate, shimmering colors transform plain white paper into pearls. The technique is simple but the effect is stunning and it is worth taking the time to make this multistrand necklace.

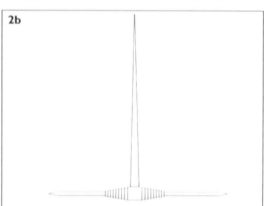

YOU WILL NEED

Thin white paper, 11¾in (297mm) wide

Craft knife and cutting mat

Toothpicks

White (PVA) glue

Knitting needle, small

Styrofoam

Several colors of pearlized pastel nail polish

SuppleMax nylon beading thread and needle

100+ clear seed beads

1 Cut the paper into isosceles triangles measuring 11¾in (297mm) long and ¾in (20mm) wide, tapering to 0in (0mm) (see page 13). This necklace uses 92 beads. The strands have 28, 30, and 33 beads respectively plus one larger linking bead.

2 Put the toothpick horizontally about ¾in (20mm) away from the fattest end of one of the triangles and gently fold the end of it, then roll the triangle into a bead, secure with glue, and let dry (see page 14). Repeat for the rest of the triangles.

3 Roll one triangle onto a knitting needle so that the center is wide enough for three threads to be threaded through. Make sure the hole is not too wide or the beads will slide inside it.

2a

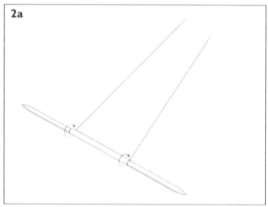

2b

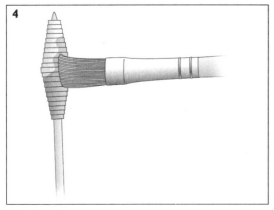

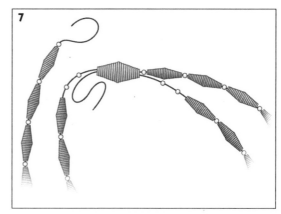

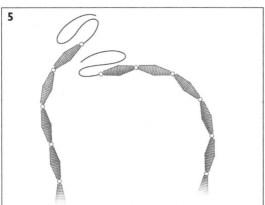

4 Paint the beads with two coats of nail polish, allowing the nail polish to dry between coats (see page 15). Try not to get nail polish on the toothpicks.

5 Starting and ending with a seed bead and leaving a tail of about 2¾in (7cm), thread on alternating seed and paper beads until the first strand of your necklace reaches the desired length. Arrange the colors randomly.

6 Thread on the larger bead. Starting and ending with two seed beads, thread alternating beads as before until you are happy with the length of the second strand.

7 Push the thread through the larger bead and make your third strand, finishing and ending with three seed beads.

8 Take the thread through the large bead, tie a secure knot with the tail, dab some glue on the knot, and tuck the excess threads back inside the surrounding beads.

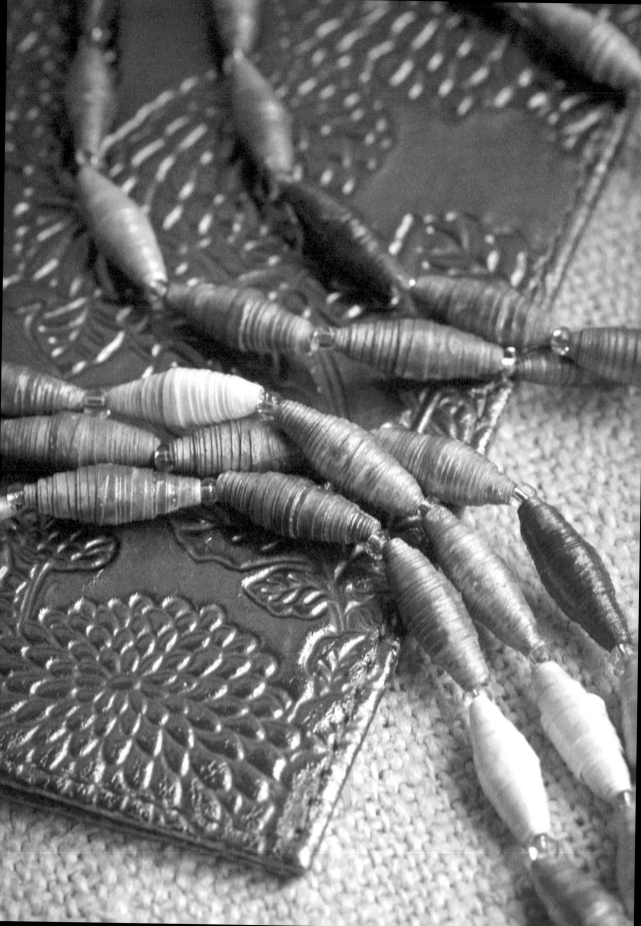

SEED PEARL RING

A cluster of lustrous pearls are topped with sparkling seed beads and joined onto a simple band. Continue adding more beads to the cluster if you want to make a larger version.

YOU WILL NEED

Thin white paper, 11¾in (297mm) wide

Craft knife and cutting mat

Toothpicks

White (PVA) glue

Styrofoam

Several colors of pearlized pastel nail polish

35½in (90cm) SuppleMax nylon beading thread and needle

35–45 clear seed beads

1 Cut the paper into isosceles triangles measuring 11¾in (297mm) long and ¾in (20mm) wide, tapering to 0in (0mm) (see page 13). This ring uses 10 paper beads. Roll each triangle into a bead and let dry (see page 14).

2 Paint the beads with two coats of nail polish (see page 15).

3 Thread the first paper bead on, leaving a tail of 2¾in (7cm), add a seed bead, and take the thread back down the paper bead.

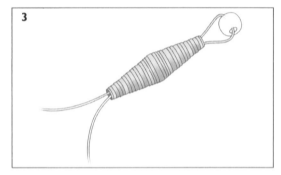

4 Thread a second paper bead, making sure you keep the 2¾in (7cm) tail, add another seed bead, and take the thread back down through the second bead. Pull on the longer thread to tighten the two beads together and they will form a "v" shape.

5 Hold the tail and the bottom of the "v" between your thumb and forefinger of your left hand. Thread on the third paper bead and its seed bead topper and slide them up to the first two beads with the thumbnail of your right hand. Continue to add the pairs of beads until you have a cluster of five.

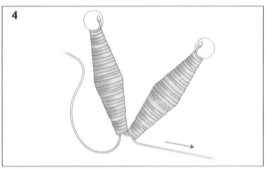

6 Holding the base of the cluster and the tail between the thumb and forefinger of your left hand, wind the long thread around the bottom of the beads and tie a single knot, left over right and under. Repeat steps 4–6 with the remaining beads. Loop the long thread around a couple of the beads, and tie a simple knot to keep the beads in position. When you have added all your beads, tie a reef knot with the tail.

7 Measure how many seed beads you need to go around your finger and thread them onto the longer thread. Take the same thread back through all the seed beads again. Pull on it to tighten the beads into a circle that touches the starburst. Tie a knot with the tail and put a dab of glue onto it. Push the excess threads back up into the beads and trim if necessary.

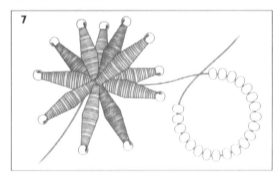

SEA URCHIN BROOCH

Spiky, spiny sea urchins were my inspiration for this piece and tissue paper is perfect for the brooch as it makes very slender beads. Different colored seed beads add that extra bit of sparkle at the tips of the spikes. It looks fantastic pinned onto a hat.

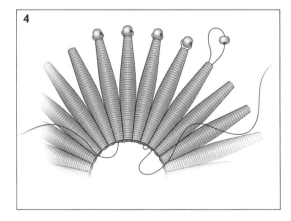

YOU WILL NEED

Tissue paper, 11¾in (297mm) wide, in different shades of orange and hot pink

Craft knife and cutting mat

Toothpicks

White (PVA) glue

Matt varnish and paintbrush

Styrofoam

SuppleMax nylon beading thread and needle

78 seed beads in oranges, copper, lime green

Cardstock

Brooch finding

1 Cut out the following number of 11¾in (297mm) long isosceles triangles (see page 13): 15 hot pink triangles that are 1⅝in (40mm) wide, tapering to 0in (0mm); 49 orange triangles that are 1⅛in (30mm) wide, tapering to 0in (0mm); 14 hot pink triangles that are ¾in (20mm) wide, tapering to 0in (0mm).

2 Roll each triangle into a bead (see page 14). Varnish twice with matt varnish and let dry.

3 Arrange 30 orange beads into spokes of a circle with a small coin-sized space in the middle. Use a coin to help if required. Each spoke must touch the one next to it. Put a line of glue on one side of the inner third of each spoke and glue it to the bead next to it. Let the glue dry.

4 Leave a 2¾in (7cm) tail and, starting in the middle, thread up through the first spoke, pick up a seed bead and bring the thread down through the same spoke into the middle, and pull gently so the seed bead sits snugly on top of the spoke. Do not pull the thread too tightly as the spokes are delicate. Take the thread up through the second spoke, pick up a seed bead, and take the thread back down through the second spoke to the middle. Add a seed bead in this way to all the spokes and tie a knot with the tail. Put a small dab of glue on the knot and hide the ends in the spokes, trimming them if necessary.

3

4

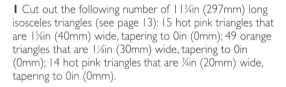

5 Arrange 15 hot pink spokes on top of the orange circle but leaving ¼in (5mm) gap away from the central hole. Place them between every other pair of orange spokes. Put a line of glue on one side of the lower third of each pink spoke. Wait a minute or two until the glue starts to go tacky. Position the spoke and press down gently on the lower third. The spoke should stand up a little as the slope of it attaches to the slope of the orange spoke underneath. Keep your finger on it until the glue sets a bit more. Glue all the spokes on and let dry.

6 Leave a 2¾in (7cm) tail and sew seed beads onto all the pink spokes as you did to the orange spokes (see step 4).

7 Arrange the final 19 orange spokes into a circle so that the ends all touch one another and there is only a ⅜in (10mm) diameter space left in the center. These spokes will stand up even more but you must wait for the glue to become tacky. It is a bit fiddly, but well worth the effort, even if you have to leave your finger on them until the glue sets enough. Use a small tube to help the spokes stand up more if you want. Add seed beads as before. Allow to dry completely.

8 Turn the shape over and put some glue on the underneath to help hold the spokes in place. Finish off by adding the remaining pink spokes in a cluster so the hole in the middle is filled completely. Add seed beads and finish off as before. Glue a circle of cardstock to the back and attach the brooch finding.

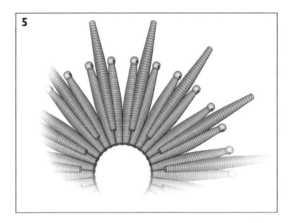

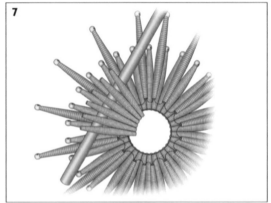

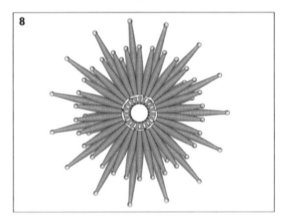

ROLLED BEAD NECKLACES

These bead necklaces use a variety of different papers and show what a wonderful range of shapes and colors can be achieved.

All of these strands are made from the same shaped equilateral triangle—11¾in (297mm) long and ¾in (20mm) wide, tapering to 0in (0mm). For instructions on how to roll your own beads, see page 14. The different papers show what variation in shape you can get and all of them are recycled. I used seed beads with some of them but they also look rather lovely on their own.

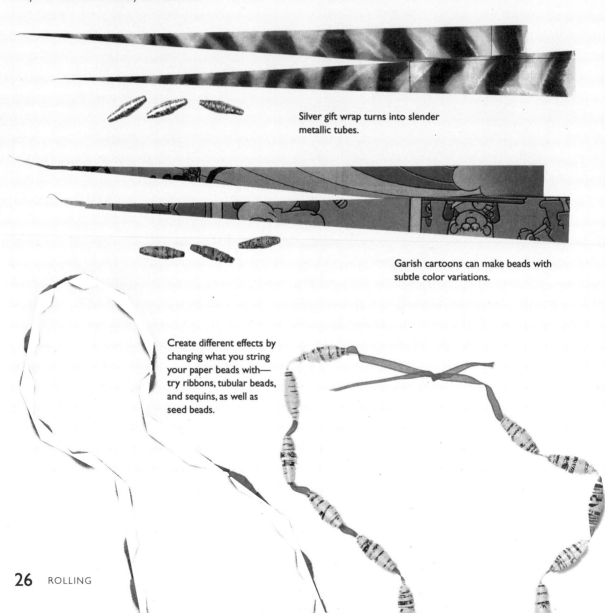

Silver gift wrap turns into slender metallic tubes.

Garish cartoons can make beads with subtle color variations.

Create different effects by changing what you string your paper beads with— try ribbons, tubular beads, and sequins, as well as seed beads.

TYPES OF PAPER USED, COUNTERCLOCKWISE FROM TOP: newspaper; construction paper with red tubular beads; black and purple metallic gift wrap; brown paper bag with orange seed beads; patterned tissue paper alternating with flower-shaped sequins; glossy magazine paper spaced with black seed beads; white and red metallic gift wrap on thin red ribbon.

WATERFALL BRACELET

Subtle color graduations give the best effect for these delicate beads and the tiny seed beads used in the bracelet suggest delicate water spray. The waterfalls are added after the bracelets are made so you can add as many or as few as you wish.

YOU WILL NEED

Elastic beading thread and needle

Tissue paper, at least 9¼in (235mm) wide, in five different shades of blue

Craft knife and cutting mat

Toothpicks

White (PVA) glue

Styrofoam

Gloss varnish and paintbrush

Five small crystal beads

60+ pale blue pearl seed beads

This bracelet is composed of five separate strands of 12 paper beads, and a waterfall of beads on each.

1 First, calculate the size of the paper beads (the size will vary according to the size of your hand). Take a length of elastic thread and wrap it around the widest part of your fist. You want to be able to pull your bracelets on without stretching the elastic too much. Measure the length of the thread and divide it by 12 to get the width of each bead. The beads used in this project are ⅝in (15mm).

2 Cut the paper into isosceles triangles measuring 9¼in (235mm) long and ⅝in (15mm) wide, tapering to 0in (0mm) (see page 13). Make at least 25 of each color. You will have some left over, which will give you some leeway in which beads you use in your bracelet.

3 Roll each triangle into a bead and let dry (see page 14).

4 Paint the beads with three coats of gloss varnish, allowing the varnish to dry between coats (see page 14).

5 Thread five strands of beads using the elastic beading thread and include one crystal bead on each, leaving a tail of 2¾in (7cm). Tie a knot at least three beads away from the crystal bead, put a dab of glue on it, and gently pull it into a bead. Trim off the ends.

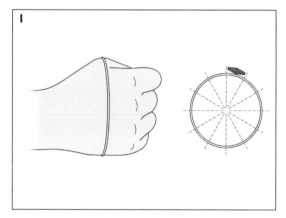

1

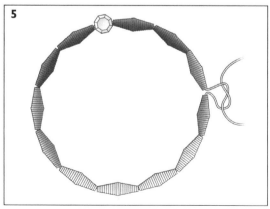

5

6 Make a waterfall of three strands of beads, alternating with the seed beads, on beading thread, and attach them to each bracelet (see diagram on page 118), or thread on as many as you want. Use a long enough piece of thread so you can thread the whole waterfall in one go. Leave a tail of 2¾in (7cm) and take the thread through the crystal bead and make the first strand of beads, beginning and ending with a seed bead. Take the thread back up through the beads and back through the crystal bead.

7 Thread on the second and third strands, as before, and through the crystal bead.

8 Finish off with a firm knot and thread any excess thread down into the beads and trim.

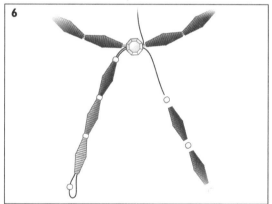

6

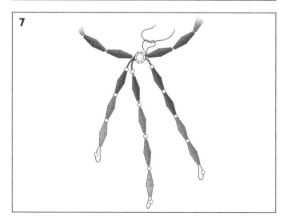

7

WATERFALL EARRINGS

A cascade of slender tissue paper beads hang gracefully down. I used color graduation from dark to light but equally you could mix the colors up.

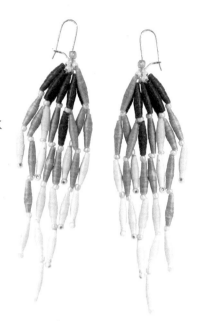

YOU WILL NEED

Tissue paper, at least 9¼in (235mm) wide, in five different shades of blue

Craft knife and cutting mat

Toothpicks

White (PVA) glue

Styrofoam

Gloss varnish and paintbrush

63in (160cm) beading thread and needle

Four small crystal beads, large enough for 16 threads to go through

82 pale blue pearl seed beads

Each earring is composed of eight strands of beads alternating with seed beads; three of three, two of four, two of five, and one of six—33 beads for each earring.

1 Cut your paper into isosceles triangles 9¼in (235mm) long and ⅝in (15mm) wide, tapering to 0in (0mm) (see page 13). Make more beads than you think you will need of each color (at least 66 beads in total). You will have some left over but it will give you some leeway in how you want the colors to fall (see diagram on page 118).

2 Roll each triangle into a bead and let dry (see page 14).

3 Paint the beads with three coats of gloss varnish, allowing it to dry properly between coats (see page 14). Remember the color of the beads will darken a little.

4 Use a long enough piece of thread so you can thread the whole waterfall in one go. Leave a tail of 2¾in (7cm) and thread the first strand of beads, beginning and ending with a seed bead. Take the thread up through two crystal beads. Bring it out over the side of the top bead, back down through the second one, and then thread on the second strand.

5 Continue to thread the strands up and down through the crystal beads as before.

6 Finish off with a firm knot and a dab of glue, thread any excess thread down into the beads, and trim. Make the other earring and attach the findings by sliding a wire into one of the crystal beads.

4

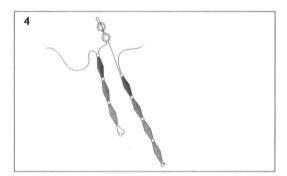

5

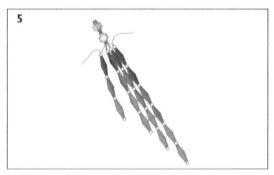

6

ICICLE EARRINGS

Even though these earrings are laden down with beads, they are still incredibly lightweight. The silvery icicles glint in the light as they move. You could add some very long strands to enhance the effect.

YOU WILL NEED

Silver gift wrap or silver patterned paper, at least 9¼in (235mm) wide

Craft knife and cutting mat

Toothpicks

White (PVA) glue

Styrofoam

Beading thread and needle

Crystal seed beads of varying sizes

Gloss varnish and paintbrush

Hooped earring findings, 1⅜in (35mm) diameter

Each earring is composed of 22 silver paper beads and approximately 100 seed beads.

1 Cut your paper into isosceles triangles measuring 9¼in (235mm) long and ¾in (20mm) wide, tapering to 0in (0mm) (see page 13). You can also use the template on page 119.

2 Roll each triangle into a bead and let dry (see page 14).

3 Paint the beads with two coats of gloss varnish, allowing it to dry between coats (see page 14).

4 Open up your earring hoop and draw the shape of it as a guide. Arrange the icicles in position around the hoop (see diagram on page 119).

5 Leave a tail of 2¾in (7cm) and tie the thread around the fixed end of the hoop, thread on two seed beads, add a silver bead, and another seed bead. Take the thread back up through the silver bead and the first two seed beads. The central holes in the icicles may vary a little so make sure the seed beads do not disappear into the icicle, just switch them for slightly larger beads if they are in danger.

6 Attach the icicles to the hoop. Decide how many seed beads you want before the next icicle, I used one, and add the bead onto the thread. Slide the hoop from right to left, through the seed bead. Pull the thread and push the beads tightly together on the hoop.

7 Continue to add icicles in this way until you have almost filled up the hoop. Remember you have to leave space for the loop to close. Tie a firm knot around the hoop after the last icicle. Add a dab of glue and trim the ends.

8 Make the other earring, mirroring the icicle arrangement, and attach findings.

5
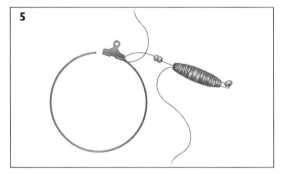

6
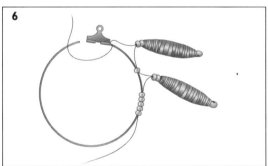

8

CHINA BRACELET

In blue and white, giving the effect of china, this bracelet is so simple and provides a great way to use up old envelopes. The bead shape is designed so that the pattern can be seen clearly. If you don't have any spare envelopes, blue ink scribbled onto white paper makes effective patterned beads, too.

YOU WILL NEED

Envelopes with blue patterns inside

White paper and blue pen (optional)

Craft knife and cutting mat

Toothpicks

White (PVA) glue

Styrofoam

Matt varnish and paintbrush

Stretch magic thread and needle

Approx. 33 seed beads in different shades of blue and white

This bracelet is composed of three strands; each strand having five large and five smaller paper beads and one extra paper bead for joining the strands, totalling 16 large paper beads and 15 smaller paper beads.

1 Use the template on page 120 and cut out and roll up at least eight large and seven small paper beads (see page 14). Coat twice with matt varnish.

2 Take a length of thread and leave a 2¾in (7cm) tail. Begin with a seed bead followed by a small paper bead and then alternate seed beads with a mixture of paper beads and end with a large bead following a small bead. Eventually, the joining bead should have seed beads next to it and smaller paper beads next to them on each side. Make sure the patterns are scattered. Thread as many beads as you need so that the length is slightly smaller than the circumference of the widest part of your hand as you pull a bracelet over it. You want to be able to pull your bracelets on without stretching the elastic too much. Try it loosely over your fist.

3 Lay the strand down on your work surface. The large bead at one end is your joining bead. Count up the beads in the remainder of the strand and multiply that by the number of strands you want. Cut out and roll up the remainder of the number of beads you need (see step 1). Lay out the beads in the order you want, beginning and ending with the smaller beads and the seed beads.

4 Cut off as much thread as you will need to make your strands in one go. Push the thread through the linking bead to create a circle and thread on the next row of beads, adding the seed beads as you go.

5 Take the thread back through the linking bead, thread on the third strand, and tie a knot with the tail to complete the circle, put a dab of glue on it, and gently pull it into a bead. Trim off the ends.

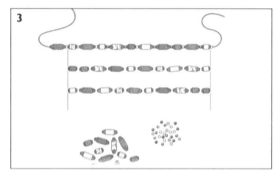

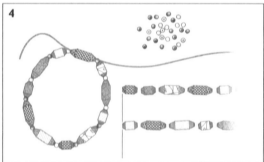

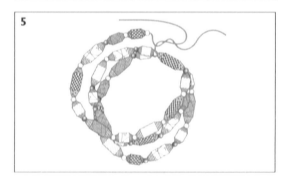

CHAPTER TWO

PAPIER MACHE

TECHNIQUES AND EQUIPMENT

Papier mâché is a wonderful medium for making jewelry and a great way to recycle old papers. Some papers will give a rougher surface than others. Of the recipes I'm giving you, paper towel gives the smoothest, shredded paper the next smoothest, and newspaper the roughest. I don't sand my beads as I like the rough texture of the paper, although I have read that some people use sandpaper on theirs. I believe that if you try and make them as smooth as possible, you might as well buy manufactured beads.

BASIC RECIPE

YOU WILL NEED

Paper

Old saucepan

Water

Blender

Sieve

White (PVA) glue

Plastic wrap (clingfilm)

Plastic, airtight container

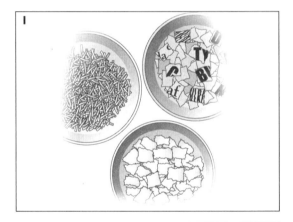

1 Tear paper into tiny pieces and place in an old saucepan. Pour on boiling water so the pieces are covered by about 4in (10cm) water and let soak overnight.

2 Bring to a boil and low boil for 30 minutes. Let cool.

3 Blend small batches in a blender with plenty of water for a couple of minutes. Make sure to keep your hand firmly on the lid and hold the blender steady because the paper will be in a big clump to begin with and the blender may jump.

4 Pour the mixture into a sieve.

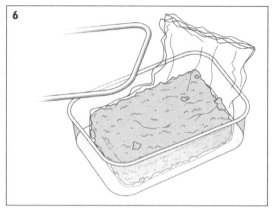

5 Squeeze out most of the liquid. Mix just enough white (PVA) glue with the pulp until the mixture can be rolled into balls which are a good, even shape and do not come apart. Don't add so much that the mixture becomes too sticky. The amount will vary depending on the paper and how much water you leave in the mixture. It's a bit like making pastry.

6 Wrap in plastic wrap. Place in an airtight plastic container in the refrigerator until you are ready to use it. This will keep for several weeks.

NEWSPAPER PULP

2oz (50g) newspaper mixed with approx. 2½oz (60g) white (PVA) glue will make approx. 25 beads of ¾in (20mm) diameter.

PAPER TOWEL PULP

10 sheets (¾oz/20g) paper towel mixed with approx. ¾oz (20g) white (PVA) glue will make approx. 15 beads of ¾in (20mm) diameter.

SHREDDED WHITE PAPER PULP

2oz (50g) cross-cut shredded paper mixed with approx. 2½oz (60g) white (PVA) glue will make approx. 25 beads of ¾in (20mm) diameter. Make sure there are no staples in the mixture.

COLORED TISSUE PAPER PULP

One sheet 20 x 27in (50 x 70cm) mixed with approx. ½oz (10g) white (PVA) glue will make approx. 6–7 beads of ¾in (20mm) diameter. This may stain your hands so wear latex gloves when handling the pulp.

FRAGRANCE

For scented beads, a few drops of essential oil, such as rose or lavender, can be worked into the pulp before you roll it into balls.

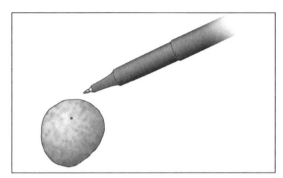

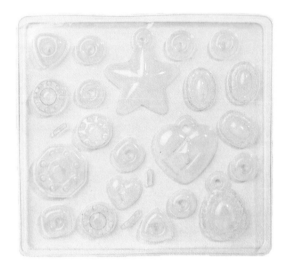

FORMING SHAPES

Roll lumps of the pulp between your palms to form balls. You can weigh the lumps to make sure the beads will be as close as possible in size or just do it by eye. The balls can then be flattened and molded into other shapes. Molds are great. You can use cookie cutters, not to cut out a shape completely but as a guide to help you to trim your project into shape. Chocolate molds are great fun as well. Anything that has a clearly defined pattern on it and won't be ruined by putting something wet on it is an option. I roll the pulp out into a thin layer between two sheets of plastic wrap first. If I'm pressing it into a deep mold, I often line the mold with a layer of plastic wrap first so I can lift the shape out easily. I always remove the shape from the mold when it is partly dry, and peel off any plastic wrap so that all of the pulp is exposed to the air.

HOLES

These can be made while the beads are wet by using a large, very sharp needle. First, mark where you want the hole to be. Then stab the needle into the bead, repeatedly, a little bit more each time, like a woodpecker at a tree trunk. Sometimes a little lump of paper may come off the far hole but you can just mold it back on. This method will blunt the needle quite quickly.

Alternatively, holes can be drilled when the bead is completely dry.

1 Position the bead on a spare piece of wood and tape it over the top with a cross made from two pieces of masking tape.

2 Mark the tape where you want to drill with a pen, then, using a sharp bradawl, make a little indent on the mark.

3 Keep your drill so the bit is vertical and drill a hole through the bead.

Remember to take into account how thick a thread you will be using and choose an appropriate bit size.

Always make a few more beads than you think you might need in case you don't drill some as accurately as you would want. You can always turn them into earrings.

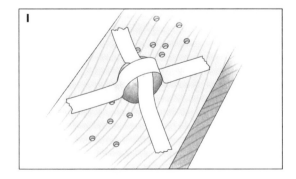

DRYING

The beads are quite heavy when they are wet but they will dry to become incredibly light. Remember that they will shrink when they dry and have a rougher texture. They can be left to dry in the air or on a fine rack on top of a warm radiator. Change their position a couple of times as they dry. If you dry them on a plastic sheet, one side will end up flat unless you rotate them. This is because their weight puts pressure on the bottom of the beads. The drying time will depend on several factors; the size of the beads, how much water they still hold, how warm the radiator, whether the weather is damp. It may take several days but don't be tempted to use them before they are completely dry. Also, don't put them anywhere too hot as the heat may warp the pulp.

PAINTING THE BEADS

I use a variety of mediums, such as acrylic, watercolor, and powder, and I am constantly trying out new ideas. Always remember to use as little water as possible when using a water-based medium. It's tempting to rush through the decorating stage but make sure your beads are perfectly dry before you paint them with anything and let them dry thoroughly between coats. If the beads have a rough texture, use a coarse brush and dab the paint on rather that trying to paint it on smoothly. That way, you'll get the paint into any little crevices.

MAKING UP A PROJECT

When you are using beads that have a very rough texture and irregular shape, they won't fit closely together and you may see some of the beading thread, especially when stringing them in a small circle. Your projects will look more finished if you use some type of spacer bead to separate your paper beads. Of course, you can always design a project where you want the thread to show! You can thread a ribbon through the holes by sewing some cotton thread onto the end of a ribbon and pulling it through the hole with that.

As with a cookery recipe, do not swap between different units of measurement when making the projects, because the conversions are not exact.

INSTANT PAPIER MACHE PULP

There are some brands of instant pulp on the market but they are quite expensive and I find it more satisfying to recycle paper whenever possible.

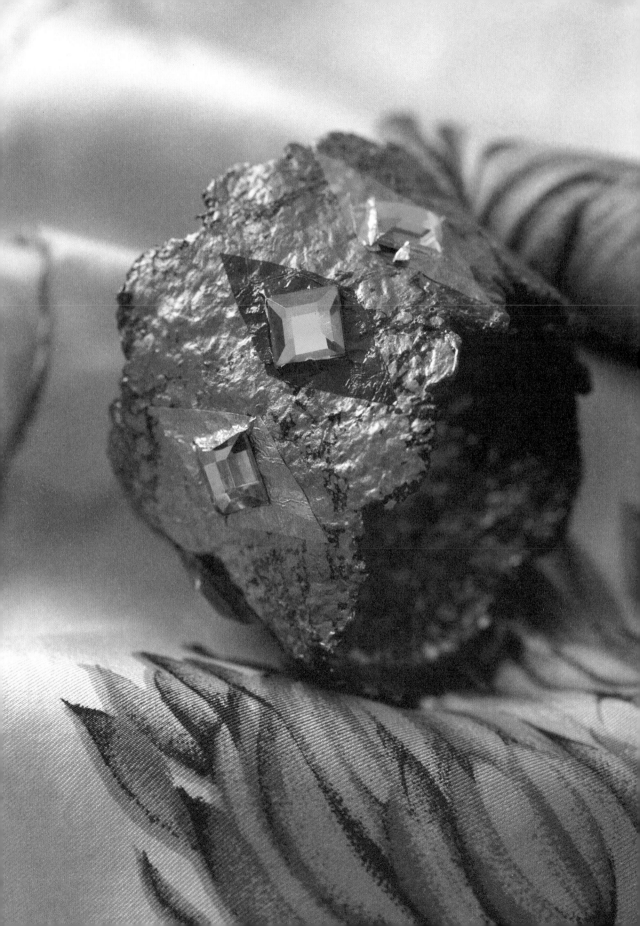

HARLEQUIN CUFF

The inspiration for this bronzed cuff studded with gems came from a Viking treasure trove. As it is so big, it needed a little extra embellishment and I added the Harlequin design. It'll definitely get people's attention.

YOU WILL NEED

Approx. ⅓ basic recipe for shredded paper pulp (see page 39)

Plastic wrap (clingfilm)

Rolling pin

Bottle or tube that is slightly large in diameter than your fist (allow for pulp to shrink a little when dry)

Dark eggplant (aubergine) latex (emulsion) paint

Paintbrushes

Popsicle (lolly) stick

Gold spray paint

Matt varnish

Paper and pencil

Flat-backed diamantés in topaz

Colored foil scraps in dark chocolate and bronze

White (PVA) glue

Scissors

Craft knife and cutting mat

1 Form the pulp into a long sausage shape and roll it out thinly between two sheets of plastic wrap. You may not need to use it all. Pay particular attention to getting some interesting edge shapes.

2 Wrap the shape around the bottle and let dry overnight, overlapping the ends a little. Carefully remove the outer layer of plastic wrap as it will probably still be quite wet.

3 When the pulp is firm to the touch on the outside, and has started to dry out a little more, gently slide it off your mold and peel off the inner plastic wrap. Let it dry out completely. The ends may start to overlap a little more.

4 Paint the shape with dark eggplant (aubergine) paint, inside and out and let it dry completely. This will make the cuff quite damp again so handle it carefully and don't put too much paint on in one go.

5 Place the cuff on a popsicle stick and spray lightly with gold paint so you get a spattered texture and can still see some of the eggplant (aubergine) color showing through.

6 Varnish twice with matt varnish. Let dry.

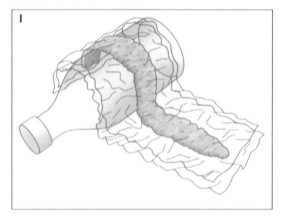

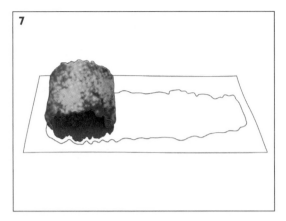

7 Plan your diamanté and diamond pattern on paper first (see template page 121). You can make a plan of your cuff by rolling it along a piece of paper and drawing along the edges.

8 Mark the position of your diamantés along the edge of a thin strip of paper and wrap it around your cuff to help you position them accurately. Use some white (PVA) glue on the cuff and on the back of the diamantés when you stick them on. Attach them to the top of the cuff a couple at a time, and let the glue dry before adding more, otherwise they may slide off. Turn the cuff round to add more.

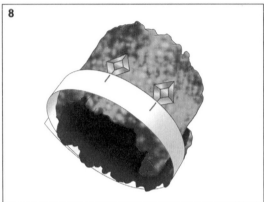

9 Make a template (see page 121) and cut out the diamond shapes from the foil paper. Cut a hole in the middle of each with a sharp craft knife that is slightly smaller than your diamantés. Smear white (PVA) glue on the back of the foil diamonds and position them over the diamantés. Ease them into position so the foil comes up the sides of the diamantés and it looks like the gems are embedded in it. Let dry.

10 Varnish with matt varnish. Let dry.

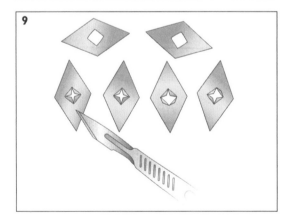

VARIATION OF HARLEQUIN CUFF
SEA BLUE BRACELET

This bracelet is a slimmer variation of the Harlequin Cuff (see page 43). I prepared the pulp for the bracelet in exactly the same way as for the cuff, only I made a slimmer sausage shape before rolling it out.

YOU WILL NEED

Approx. ⅓ basic recipe for shredded paper pulp (see page 39)

Plastic wrap (clingfilm)

Rolling pin

Bottle or tube that is slightly larger in diameter than your fist (allow for pulp to shrink some when dry)

Powder paints in a variety of blues and a stiff brush

Lollipop stick

Matt varnish and paintbrush

Scraps of tissue paper in blues

Scrap paper or chocolate wrapper in silvery blue

Motif or hole punch

White (PVA) glue

Flat-backed diamantés

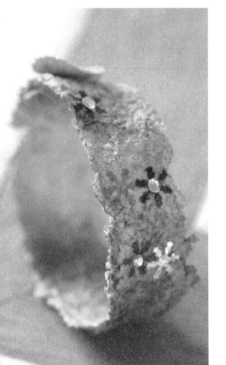

1 Form the pulp into a slim sausage shape and roll it out thinly between two sheets of plastic wrap. You may not need to use it all. Pay particular attention to getting some interesting edge shapes.

2 Follow steps 2–3 as for the Harlequin Cuff (see page 43).

3 Use a stiff brush and dab the powder paints over the bracelet until it is completely covered. Make sure you get the color into all the crevices. Tap off any excess powder.

4 Varnish twice with matt varnish. Let dry.

5 Punch motifs in different colored tissue paper and chocolate wrappers. The easiest way to do this is to punch several layers at a time or put the tissue paper on top of a sheet of white paper. Apply a very thin layer of white (PVA) glue to them and stick them randomly onto the outside surface of the bracelet. Use a toothpick to help you if you need to. Let dry.

6 Apply some flat-backed diamantés around the bracelet. Use some white (PVA) glue on the cuff and on the back of the diamantés when you stick them on and wait until the glue is a little tacky before pressing them firmly into place. Only apply a few at a time.

7 Varnish with matt varnish. Let dry.

SPARKLE FLOWER BROOCH

This would be a terrific project to make with kids as it's so simple. You are limited only by your cookie cutters. Try doing some color sketches first before deciding on the final design.

YOU WILL NEED

Approx. ⅓ basic recipe for shredded paper pulp (see page 39)

Plastic wrap (clingfilm)

Rolling pin

Cookie cutters (optional— see step 2)

Scissors

Acrylic paint in white, cadmium yellow, and cadmium red

Paintbrushes

Mixing plate

Matt varnish

White (PVA) glue

Flat-backed diamantés in pink and green

Brooch finding

1 Roll the pulp out thinly between two sheets of plastic wrap. You will have enough to make several shapes.

2 Remove the top layer of plastic wrap and press the cookie cutter firmly into the pulp. It will not go through the pulp completely. Leave the shapes on the bottom layer of plastic wrap. Let dry a little. (If you do not have a cookie cutter in the shape you want, you could draw your shapes freehand by pressing a blunt knife into the pulp—or see template on page 122.)

3 When the pulp is firm enough to be picked up without bending, peel it off the plastic wrap. Use a sharp pair of scissors and cut out using the shape indentation as a guide. Let dry.

4 Paint the shape, back and front, and let dry.

5 Varnish the shape back and front and, while it is drying, draw the shape on a piece of spare paper and practice arranging your diamantés in the pattern you want to use. When the varnish has dried, glue the diamantés on one at a time.

6 Finish by attaching the brooch finding with white (PVA) glue.

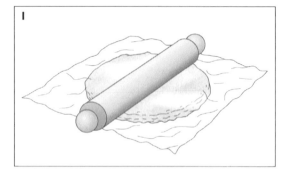

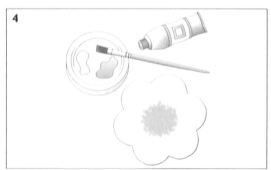

BLING BROOCHES

Just like the Sparkle Flower Brooch (see page 48), all these brooches are easy to make and are a great way to add a splash of color to any outfit.

I used shredded paper pulp for all of these brooches (see page 39). I rolled the pulp out flat between two sheets of plastic wrap. and then I used cookie cutters to press firmly into the pulp. (If you want to create these shapes without cookie cutters, the templates are on page 122.)

I peeled off the top layer of wrap and left it to dry. When it was almost dry, I took the shapes off of the bottom sheet so that side could dry properly and cut around the guidelines with some scissors. Then I used a mixture of sequins and diamantés to decorate them.

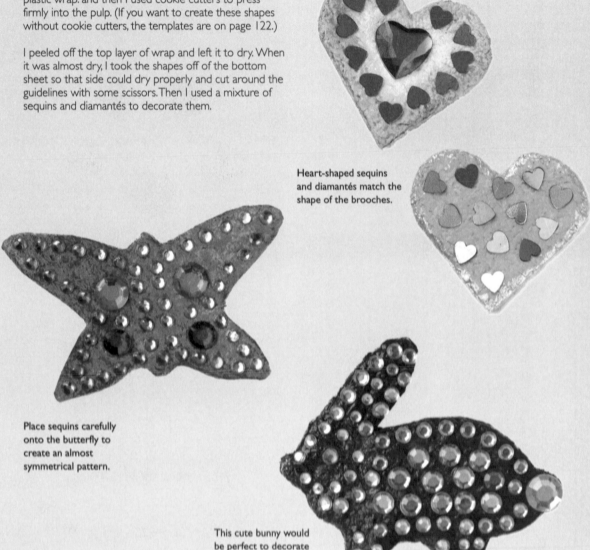

Heart-shaped sequins and diamantés match the shape of the brooches.

Place sequins carefully onto the butterfly to create an almost symmetrical pattern.

This cute bunny would be perfect to decorate a little girl's coat or bag.

RED VELVET NECKLACE

This necklace demonstrates that the stringing material can be an integral part of your design. This fine, velvet, red ribbon emphasizes the soft effect I wanted to achieve.

YOU WILL NEED

Basic recipe tissue paper pulp— two recipes using dark red, ⅔ recipe using bright red tissue paper (see page 39)

Large, sharp needle or drill (see page 40)

Matt varnish and paintbrush

Approx. 40in (1m) very thin velvet ribbon

Scissors

String

Toothpick

White (PVA) glue

1 Divide the dark red and the bright red papier mâché pulp into approx. 14 pieces in each color, leaving a tiny amount over. (This is more than you will need, in case you drill the holes incorrectly.) Combine one lump of each color and roll into balls. Keep the brighter red on one side so you can see the difference between the colors. Flatten them slightly into button shapes. Roll three tiny balls from the leftover lump, approx. ⅜in (10mm) diameter, but don't flatten. Pierce holes through the widest part of the beads (or wait until beads are completely dry before drilling if you prefer). Check that the holes are large enough for the thread to go through (see page 40). Let dry, then varnish several times with matt varnish.

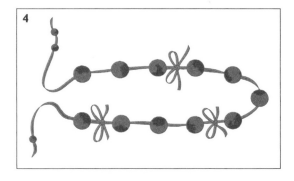

2 Cut three 6in (16cm) pieces of ribbon for the necklace bows. Plan the length of your necklace by tying a piece of string into a circle as a guide, checking you can pull it over your head easily. My circle was 27in (68cm). Arrange the string into a long oval on your work surface and space out as many large beads as you want to check how they will look. I used 11, placing one at the bottom of the necklace, and allowed approx. 1⅜in (35mm) between each bead. Arrange your ribbon next to the string. Leave one end of the ribbon three times as long as the other but allow enough on both ends to tie the closing bow.

3 Thread the beads onto the ribbon. Keep the beads flat on the work surface. Move each bead left by ¾in (10mm). Dab some white (PVA) glue onto the ribbon to the right of each bead. Slide the bead ¾in (10mm) to the right and over the glued ribbon. Don't put a huge amount of glue on as it will not go inside the bead. Do the same with every bead. Let dry.

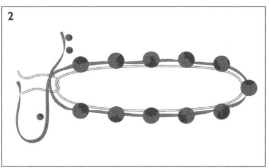

4 Tie the three small ribbon lengths into bows onto your necklace between the beads. Trim the ends of the ribbon at an angle, then thread two small beads onto one end and one small bead onto the other, gluing the ribbon as before. Tie the ends into a bow to fasten.

RED VELVET BRACELET

This is the simplest of bracelets to make, with the beads strung onto elastic thread so you can just pull it on. If you add an extra touch like this ribbon bow, it takes the design to a new level.

YOU WILL NEED

Basic recipe tissue paper pulp—one recipe using dark red, $\frac{1}{3}$ recipe using a bright red tissue paper (see page 39)

Large, sharp needle or drill (see page 40)

Matt varnish and paintbrush

Approx. 13in (33cm) clear Stretch Magic elastic thread and needle

Red seed beads

9½in (24cm) very thin velvet ribbon

Scissors

Toothpick

White (PVA) glue

1 Divide the dark red and the bright red papier mâché pulp into approx. 11 pieces in each color and leave a tiny bit over. This is more than you will need, as you need some spare in case you drill the holes incorrectly.

2 Combine one lump of each color and roll into balls. Try to keep the brighter red on one side so you can see the difference between the colors. Flatten them slightly into button shapes. Roll two tiny balls from the leftover lump, approx ⅜in (10mm) diameter but don't flatten. Pierce holes through the widest part of the beads (or wait until beads are completely dry before drilling if you prefer). Check the holes are large enough for the thread to go through. Let dry.

3 Varnish several times with matt varnish. Let dry.

4 Thread the papier mâché beads, alternating with red seed beads, onto the elastic thread to check that your bracelet will be the right size. The finished circumference should be slightly smaller than the circumference of the widest part of your hand as you pull a bracelet over it. You can add or subtract a bead or two if necessary.

5 Tie a square knot. Put a dot of white (PVA) glue onto the knot and pull the beads along gently so the knot slides into the hole of one of the papier mâché beads.

6 Trim the ends of the ribbon at an angle. Thread a small round bead onto each end. Move them to one side slightly, smear a little white (PVA) glue onto the ribbon next to them, and reposition them over the glue. Let dry.

7 Tie the ribbon into a bow between the two beads where you tied the knot.

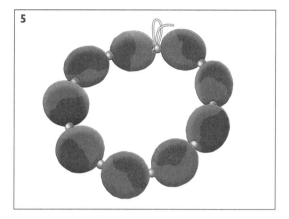

MOSSY BEAD NECKLACE

I was imagining rock pools and tiny, round pebbles encrusted with lichen and moss when I designed these beads. Unlike some beads this size, these featherweight ones will not pull on your neck and weigh you down.

YOU WILL NEED

Approx. one basic recipe for paper towel pulp (see page 39)

Large, sharp needle or drill (see page 40)

Old eye shadow or powder paints and stiff brush

Motif or hole punch

Scraps of tissue paper or candy wrappers in assorted colors

White (PVA) glue

Toothpicks

Matt varnish and paintbrush

45in (114cm) cotton cord

Masking tape

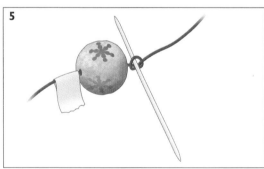

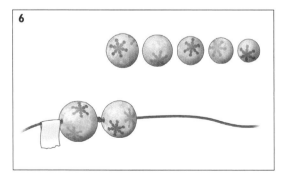

1 Divide the pulp into lumps of graduating sizes and roll into balls (see page 40). I made 14 balls, two of each size, plus one larger ball for a central bead of ½oz (14g) and one spare ball from the leftovers to practice with. Let dry and make a hole in them large enough for the thread to go through (see page 40).

2 Use the brush and dab patches of different colored greens onto the beads. Don't rub the surface too much or you will make it wooly. Shake off any excess powder. Punch some of your motifs in different colored tissue paper. The easiest way to do this is to punch several layers at a time or put the tissue paper on top of a sheet of white paper. Apply a very thin layer of white (PVA) glue to them and stick them onto the beads randomly. Let dry.

3 Varnish twice with matt varnish and let dry.

4 Arrange your beads in a line, starting with one of the smallest, increasing in size until you get the largest, central bead and then decreasing in size until you finish with the smallest.

5 Start to thread the beads. Position the largest bead in the middle of your cord. Put a little bit of masking tape to the left of it so it won't move in that direction. Tie a loose, simple knot to the right of the bead by making a loop of right over left and bringing the cord up through the middle. Put a toothpick in the middle of the knot and move it closer to the bead. When you have positioned the knot where you want it, pull on the cord to tighten it, and pull out the toothpick.

6 Add half of the remaining beads, tying a knot between them, in descending size order and finish with a knot. Remove the masking tape and treat the other half of the necklace in the same way. Tie the cord in a bow to the length you want.

MOSSY BEAD RING

This is a ring to get you noticed. You could make a huge one of these and it would still be very comfortable to wear. It looks particularly attractive if you can match the seed beads to the color of the paper bead. Practice drilling your holes on some spare beads first so you are confident when drilling.

YOU WILL NEED

1 mossy bead, approx. 1 in (25mm) diameter (see page 56)

Large, sharp needle or drill (see page 40)

Small dark red and moss green beads

18in (45cm) SuppleMax nylon beading thread and needle

1 Make the mossy bead (see page 56).

2 Drill two holes through the bead as close as possible to where the bead will sit on your finger (see page 40). Measure around your finger to decide how large the bead circle should be.

3 Make a length of small green beads with a larger red bead at each end and another larger red bead six beads away from each end.

4 Leave a small tail at one end and push the other end of the thread through one set of holes in the mossy bead. Form a circle by threading it through the next 10 beads on the other side of the hole.

5 Miss one bead and go back through one green and one red bead. Thread on six green beads and one red bead, push the thread through the mossy bead, and add one red bead and six green beads. Go through the next three beads. Miss one bead and bring the thread back through one green and one red bead.

6 Take the thread up through the beads to join with the tail and tie a firm knot. Add a dab of glue to the knot, trim, and push the ends into the beads.

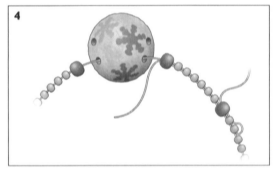

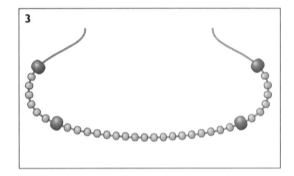

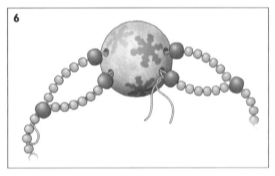

BIG BOULDER RINGS

These statement rings are similar to the Mossy Bead Ring (see page 58)—
because they're made from papier mâché, they're lighter than store-bought
rings of this size.

I used paper towel pulp for all of these rings (see page 39). When I had made the balls to the sizes I wanted, I dropped them onto a plastic sheet from a couple of feet above it. This gave them all a flat bottom. I molded the bottoms a little more by pressing them gently onto my fingers. You have to be careful not to destroy the round shape of the top of the bead though so be gentle.

With these rings, it is best if holes are drilled when they are dry (see page 40). When you are drilling to make a bead circle that comes in from the side, try to drill the holes close to the part of the bead that will be on your finger and not through the center.

Thread a string of seed beads through to make the actual ring, tie a knot near a hole, and put a dab of glue on the knot. Trim the ends and hide them in the beads. You can also use a top to bottom hole. When you use this, you will have to hide the hole at the top with a bead or sequin. I used SuppleMax thread.

SHINY IVORY ROSE

I thought this would make a pretty ring so the design needed to be simple. I drilled a hole either side, painted the bead with shiny, pearlized, ivory nail polish, and glued a cutout découpage miniature rose onto the top. I wanted an extremely shiny finish so I varnished it several times with découpage gloss varnish. I used pearly seed beads for the bead circle with two bigger beads to hide the side holes a little.

BUTTERFLY

I decided to glue miniature butterfly découpage motifs onto this one and thought it might look better if it moved around a little, so I drilled a top to bottom hole. I painted it with dark blue gouache and left it to dry completely before giving it two coats of matt varnish. Then I stuck the butterfly motifs on and varnished them with découpage gloss varnish. I left the front wings of the top butterfly unglued and positioned it so the bead looks like the head. I used small dark blue beads for the bead circle and finished the circle by taking the thread through the first bead, in the opposite direction. I left one end as a tail and took the thread up through the paper bead, added on a blue bead and brought the thread back down through the paper bead to fasten a knot with the tail end. I added a dab of glue to the knot, trimmed the ends, and hid them in the beads.

GLITTERBALL

Because I wanted to use diamanté, I wanted a bit of movement on this, and I drilled a top to bottom hole. I painted it with purple gouache and let it dry before varnishing it with two coats of matt varnish. I wanted a delicate bead circle so I used some tiny silver beads. As they were very tiny, I had to use a flat sequin on the top and bottom to hide the holes. I made the bead circle and completed it by taking the thread through the first bead, in the opposite direction. I left one end as a tail and took the thread up through the paper bead, added on a flat sequin and a silver bead, and brought the thread back down through the paper bead to fasten a knot with the tail end. I added a dab of glue to the knot, trimmed the ends, and hid them in the beads. I finished it off by gluing flat diamantés over it.

PINK SEQUIN

Another tiny ring so, again, I kept the decoration simple. I drilled a hole either side, painted it with two coats of matt dusky pink nail polish and glued a sequin topped with a flat, pink diamanté on the top. The holes need to be hidden so I used two more sequins on either end of the bead ring. I found some pretty two-toned seed beads which worked perfectly for this.

FOOL'S GOLD BRACELET

I wanted these pieces to be slightly irregular so the light would catch the odd gleam of a seam of gold. Use matt varnish to enhance the contrast.

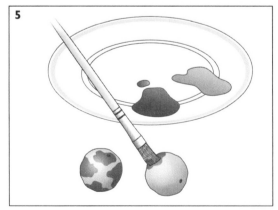

YOU WILL NEED

Approx. ⅓ basic recipe for newspaper pulp (see page 39)

Large, sharp needle or drill (see page 40)

8 gold beads

Clear Stretch Magic elastic thread and needle

Acrylic paint in burnt sienna and white

Paintbrush

Mixing plate

Scrap of gold paper approx. 2⅜in (60mm) square (reuse old candy or chocolate wrappers)

Scissors

Toothpick

White (PVA) glue

Matt varnish

1 Divide the newspaper pulp into pieces and roll into balls of approx. ¾in (20mm) diameter (see page 40). You should have 8–10 balls.

2 Let dry completely. Mark the beads with a pen and then make a hole in them large enough for the thread to go through (see page 40).

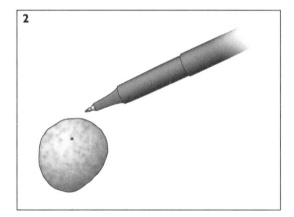

3 Thread the papier mâché beads and the alternating gold beads onto the elastic thread to check that your bracelet will be the right size. The finished circumference should be slightly smaller than the circumference of the widest part of your hand as you pull a bracelet over it. You can add or subtract a bead or two if necessary. Unthread the beads.

4 Mix two different earth shades on your plate, with a little bit of water, using your burnt sienna and white acrylic paints. One color should be quite dark and the other a mid-tone. Do not use too much water as, remember, you'll be painting onto paper.

5 Paint half of each bead randomly with each color. It is better to dab the paint on as the bead's surface is uneven and you need to make sure the paint covers it all. Let dry.

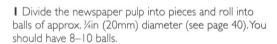

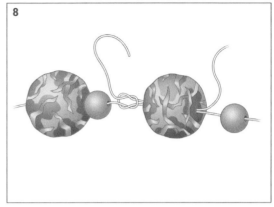

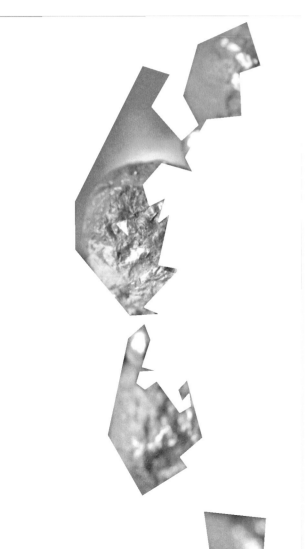

6 Cut shards of gold paper, smear some white (PVA) glue on the back of them, and, using a toothpick to help you, position them roughly onto the beads and then press them down more firmly with a finger when you are happy with their position. Try to alter their angles so each bead looks different and the gold follows some of the ridges in the beads like a gold seam in a mine. Let dry.

7 Varnish with matt varnish and let dry.

8 Rethread all the beads. Tie a square knot. Put a dot of white (PVA) glue onto the knot and pull the beads along gently so the knot slides into the hole of one of the papier mâché beads.

VARIATION OF FOOL'S GOLD BRACELET

FOOL'S GOLD RING

This was an experiment to see if I needed to use a metal or card ring for a base, and I didn't! The Flintstones may have had rings just like this. It would also look fab with a huge gem embedded in it.

YOU WILL NEED

Tube the same circumference as your finger

Strip of scrap paper

Small piece of plastic wrap (clingfilm)

Newspaper pulp for approx. two beads of ¾in (20mm) diameter (see page 39)

Acrylic paint in burnt sienna and white

Paintbrush

Mixing plate

Scrap of gold paper approx. ⅜in (10mm) square (reuse old candy or chocolate wrappers)

Scissors

Toothpick

White (PVA) glue

Matt varnish

1 Make a ring from a strip of scrap paper around the tube and then test the paper strip on your finger to check whether the ring will be the correct size. Remember, the papier mâché can shrink a little when drying.

2 Cover a little of the tube with a piece of plastic wrap near to one end.

3 Mold half your papier mâché into a long sausage, start to wrap it around the tube near one end, and flatten it with your fingers. Form the remainder of the papier mâché into a ball and join it onto the ring you have made. Continue to mold it until you have a good shape. Leave until just starting to dry, and remove from the tube by pulling gently on the plastic wrap. Let dry.

4 Mix two different earth shades on your plate, with a little bit of water, using the burnt sienna and white acrylic paints. One color should be quite dark and the other a mid-tone. Do not use too much water as, remember, you'll be painting onto paper.

5 Paint half of the ring randomly with each color. It is better to dab the paint on as the bead's surface is uneven and you need to make sure the paint covers it all. Let dry.

6 Cut shards of gold paper, smear some white (PVA) glue on the back of them, and, using a toothpick to help you, position them roughly onto the ring and then press them down more firmly with a finger when you are happy with their position. Try and alter their angles so the gold follows some of the ridges in the papier mâché, like a gold seam in a mine. Let dry.

7 Varnish with matt varnish and let dry.

GLOSSY RED ROSE BROOCH

Keep your eyes open for a suitable mold to make a brooch like this. I used a mirror for this mold but small cake molds would be perfect, too. Make sure whatever you use has deep indentations for a really good 3D effect. This project is great for using up leftover pulp.

YOU WILL NEED

Approx. ¼ basic recipe for shredded white paper pulp (see page 39)

Plastic mold

Cotton swab (optional)

Plastic wrap (clingfilm) (optional)

Acrylic paint in white and red

Paintbrush

Matt varnish

Dark red nail polish

Brooch finding

White (PVA) glue

1 Roll out the shredded white paper pulp and push it into the mold, making sure you press it well down into the indentations.

2 Add a small mound of pulp with a flat top to the middle of the back of the brooch with your fingers or a cotton swab. This will make the brooch stand away from your clothes a little and it will be easier to fasten and unfasten the pin.

3 Leave until just starting to dry and peel the pulp away from the mold. Let dry completely. If you are using a deep mold, you might want to line the mold with plastic wrap first so the papier mâché shape will be easier to remove.

4 Paint the rose with white acrylic paint. Let dry.

5 Paint on top of the white with the bright red acrylic paint. Let dry.

6 Once the paint has dried completely, varnish with two coats of matt varnish.

7 When dry, paint some of the petal indentations with a glossy dark red nail polish to give a 3D effect. Let dry.

8 Finish by attaching the brooch finding onto the mound on the back of the brooch with white (PVA) glue.

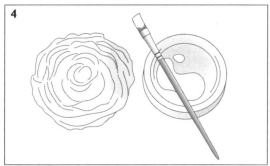

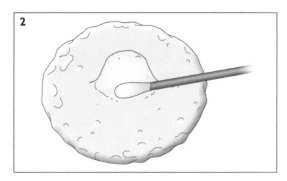

CHAPTER THREE

QUILLING

TECHNIQUES AND EQUIPMENT

Arranging coiled strips of paper into patterns has been a pastime for centuries. Today, you can buy special tools and pre-cut paper strips in an amazing riot of colors or cut your own paper and use toothpicks and thin tubes.

PAPER STRIPS

A little goes a long way and you can buy the paper strips in packs of single colors or multiple colors, which often have themes such as Summer or Winter. Generally, the strips come in three widths: ⅛in (3mm); ¼in (5mm); and ⅜in (10mm), though there may be others available. If you are accurate with a craft knife, you can cut them lengthwise into any width you want. There are also different lengths—I've come across two, 18in (45cm) and 24in (60cm), and one importer told me he had seen others, but you can cut them widthwise into shorter pieces or extend the length by adding on another strip.

Trying to choose colors is like being in a chocolate shop when you are a chocaholic. There is every color you could ever want and they have such wonderful names such as cosmic pink and denim blue. Then there are different finishes and effects—pearlized, glitter, two-tone, fringed.

MAKING YOUR OWN STRIPS

You must be accurate when you cut your strips and it's best to use a very sharp craft knife or scalpel and cutting mat. You can try this technique with all sorts of papers but some are more suitable than others and you'll learn by experimenting which you prefer. Try using plain as well as printed. You will only get a strong color if you use paper that has dye saturated through it. If you use paper that has been printed with color, the edge will be white and pale.

A gorgeous array of assorted blue and green quilling paper.

MAKING COILS INTO PROJECTS

Sometimes, it's better to use a base made from wide paper strips. If a piece has to stand up for example, like a tiara, the wider base will make it more stable. Some papers seem to have a natural curl and I always curl with it. Unless I'm adding another color on or extending the length of my paper strip, I tear the end to give a softer finish.

Arrange your coils into the design of your finished piece before you glue them into position. Remove a couple of coils at a time and glue those before pushing back into position. Generally the coils are quite robust and can be squeezed into position. Open coils may continue to open a little more over time.

Make sure to glue the coil where the end of the coil is hidden so it looks as neat as possible.

I varnish my pieces several times as it protects them and helps to strengthen them. I always check to make sure the colors don't bleed before I coat them though. Also, take care not to saturate open coils with varnish as it may make the rings clump together.

Closed coils will probably have a small hole in the middle and I usually sew tiny seed beads onto them if the back of the piece won't be seen.

As with a cookery recipe, do not swap between different units of measurement when making the projects, because the conversions are not exact.

CHANGING COLOR AND EXTENDING LENGTH

On a closed coil, make sure that both ends of the strips are perfectly straight and at right angles to their length. Finish the first strip by gluing the end down, put a small dab of glue after it, and then butt the edge of the new strip right up to it, tightly. Hold for a few seconds for the glue to start to set and then carry on with your coil.

EQUIPMENT

Not all of the below are necessary. Sometimes, I use a toothpick and size my coils by eye.

Toothpick
Styrofoam
Quilling tool—split needle (plastic or metal)
Plastic shape template or circle guide
Finepoint glue dispenser
White (PVA) glue
Varnish
Small tubes in various diameters

Three quilling tools (from top to bottom): a toothpick, a metal tool, and a split needle.

These orange and red coils can be arranged into a multitude of flower shapes.

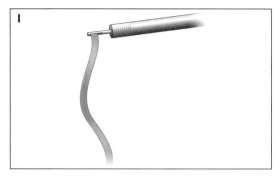

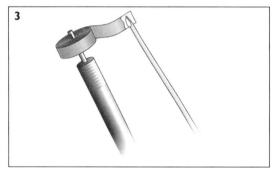

MAKING A CLOSED COIL

I Insert the very tip of your paper strip into the slot in your quilling tool, keeping it square.

2 Use an even pressure, and, while holding onto the strip with one hand, roll the tool away from or toward you. It's your preference as to which direction you roll. Keep the paper strip straight and align it on top of the coil as much as possible. Don't worry if it goes a little out of line as you can push it gently back into position.

3 Stop rolling when you have ⅜in (10mm) of strip left. Put a dab of glue on the end and continue rolling the tail end in. Use your thumb and forefinger to put a little pressure on the coil to help the glue to set.

4 Place the coil flat down onto a work surface and tap it with something flat, such as a ruler, to make the coil as flat as possible.

If you are making a closed coil without a quilling tool, use a knitting needle or small tube. Use the same technique as for a closed coil but use your fingers and thumb to roll it onto the tube to begin with.

MAKING AN OPEN COIL

You can decide how open you want your coils to be (see opposite). To do this, make a closed coil, but do not glue it. Then place it on your work surface and it will uncoil itself. You can pick it up any time and glue the end down. You can do this by eye or you can use a circle guide if it's essential that your circles are consistent.

SHAPING QUILLED COILS

Pinching quilled coils with your fingertips and nails or using tweezers to squeeze them can produce a variety of shapes, as seen in the diagrams below. I generally use my nails to make my shapes, but experiment to work out which method you prefer. Make sure you always make extra coils in case you accidentally spoil some. When you get used to making them, you will notice that the closed coils don't change shape very much at all.

I used 24in (60cm) strips for all of these coils. The scrolls and hearts are made by folding or bending the paper strip in half, rolling one end down toward the fold, and then rolling the other. The coils can be glued a little to preserve the shape.

1 QUILL—CLOSED COIL

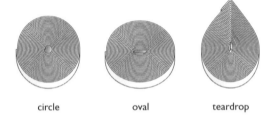

circle   oval   teardrop

1 QUILL WITH A SMALL CENTER HOLE QUILLED AROUND A THIN KNITTING NEEDLE

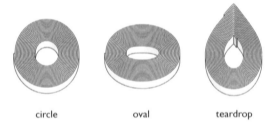

circle   oval   teardrop

OPEN COILS: THE SMALLER THE LENGTH USED, THE MORE OPEN THE COIL WILL BE

½ quill   ⅓ quill   ¼ quill

¼ QUILL—OPEN COIL PINCHED INTO DIFFERENT SHAPES

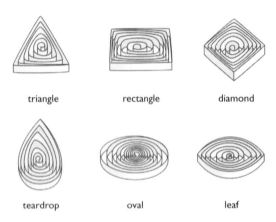

triangle   rectangle   diamond

teardrop   oval   leaf

⅓ QUILL—FOLDED IN HALF AND BOTH ENDS ROLLED DOWN TOWARD THE FOLD

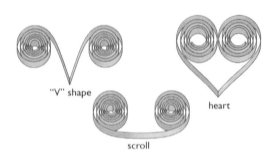

"V" shape   heart

scroll

1 QUILL ROUND A SMALL TUBE

POP ART RING

This retro homage to the psychedelic age is easier to make than it looks. Just make sure the circles are positioned very closely together.

YOU WILL NEED

Pencil and paper

⅛in (3mm) wide strips of quilling paper in black, orange, canary yellow, and lemon yellow

Quilling tool or toothpick

White (PVA) glue

Matt varnish and paintbrush

Toothpick

8 seed beads: 4 black, 4 yellow

Light, clear thread and needle

Tube that is the same diameter as your finger

Small piece of heavy cardstock in yellow

Scissors

I Plan the pattern of the ring on paper first. This has a larger central circle, surrounded by different-sized circles. Draw a slightly smaller circle than your pattern plan for the base. Make sure none of the base shape will show (see diagram on page 123).

2 Make the round shapes using a different mix of colors for each circle (see page 71). Quill seven closed coils in slightly different sizes and one larger one for the center (see page 72). Coat the circles twice with matt varnish, allowing it to dry between coats, and then dry completely.

3 Arrange the shapes in position on the pattern plan. Pull them away from each other a little and, one at a time, using a little white (PVA) glue on the end of a toothpick, put some glue on any surface that touches another circle. Push them back into position and gently squeeze them together to help the glue set. Let dry.

4 Make sure the seed beads are larger than the central holes in the quilled shapes. Leave a tail and bring the thread from the back of your shape, up through the small central hole in the middle circle, add on a contrasting color bead, and bring the thread back down through the central hole. Bring the needle up again through the central hole of the nearest circle, add on a contrasting color bead, and go back down through the central hole again. Continue to add one bead to each of the remaining circles in this way. Tie the threads in a knot at the back to finish and put a small dab of glue on the knot. Trim the thread.

5 Use a tube that is the same diameter as the finger on which you'll wear the ring. Quill two circles of two lengths of paper around the tube (see page 73), remove them, and glue them together. Varnish twice with matt varnish. Let dry.

6 Cut out the heavy cardstock base and glue the ring onto it. When it is dry, glue the finished shape onto it.

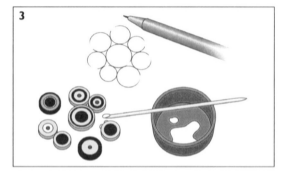

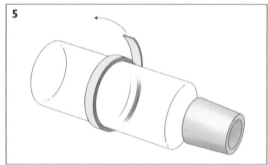

VARIATION OF POP ART RING
DIAMOND RING

Geometric shapes such as this diamond are great for rings as they are very dramatic and noticeable.

YOU WILL NEED

Paper and pencil

⅛in (3mm) wide strips of quilling paper in bright pink, dull pink, and mauve

Quilling tool or toothpick

White (PVA) glue

Matt varnish and paintbrush

Toothpick

11 mauve seed beads

Light, clear thread and sewing needle

Small piece of heavy cardstock in mauve

Tube that is the same diameter as your finger

Scissors

1 Plan the size and pattern on paper first. This pattern has three larger circles surrounded by different-sized circles. Draw a diamond for the base that is slightly smaller than your pattern plan. Make sure none of the base shape will show when the circles are stuck onto it (see template on page 123).

2 Quill eight closed coils in a mix of colors (see page 71) and slightly different sizes and three larger ones for the center line (see page 72).

3 Coat the circles twice with matt varnish, allowing it to dry between coats, and then let dry completely.

4 Arrange your shapes in position on your pattern plan. Pull them away from each other a little and, one at a time, using a little white (PVA) glue on the end of a toothpick, put some glue on any surface that touches another circle. Push them back into position and gently squeeze them together to help the glue set. Let dry.

5 Make sure your beads are larger than the central holes in your quilled shapes. Leave a tail and bring the thread from the back of your shape, up through the small central hole in the middle circle, add on a bead, and bring the thread back down through the central hole. Bring the needle up again through the central hole of the nearest circle, add on a bead, and go back down through the central hole again. Continue to add one bead to each of the remaining circles in this way. Tie the threads in a knot at the back to finish and put a small dab of glue on the knot. Trim the thread.

6 Use a tube that is the same diameter as the finger you want the ring for. Quill two circles of two lengths of paper each tightly around the tube (see page 73), remove them, and glue them together. Varnish twice with matt varnish and let dry.

7 Cut out the heavy cardstock base and glue the ring onto it. When it is dry, glue the finished shape onto it.

GREEN DAISY EARRINGS

Fresh, springlike colors made up into a simple daisy design really brightens a gray day. Ring the changes with a version in classic white with a pale pink outer edge.

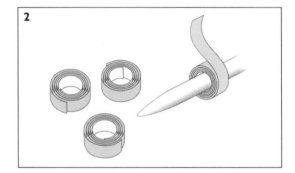

YOU WILL NEED

⅛in (3mm) wide strips of quilling paper: 8 light green, 7 mid-green, 5 mid-blue, 2 yellow

Craft knife and cutting mat

Knitting needle, medium size

Quilling tool or toothpick

White (PVA) glue

Toothpick

Matt varnish and paintbrush

Colored cardstock

Scissors

Findings: studs for pierced ears or clipons

1 Cut the light and mid-green quilling strips into halves and cut the blue strips into thirds (see page 70).

2 Make seven closed coils with a wide central hole using your knitting needle, each one using light green, continuing with mid-green, and finishing with blue (see pages 71–72).

3 Squeeze each petal into an oval.

4 Quill one closed coil for the flower center using your quilling tool or toothpick. Use the yellow first and finish it off with a light green half strip (see pages 70–72). Alternatively, make a flower center in the same colors as the petals—starting with light-green, continuing with mid-green, and finishing with blue.

5 Position the petals around the flower center on your work surface (see diagram on page 123). Pick the petals up one at a time and, using a toothpick, put a small dab of glue on the places where they touch another quill. Push them into place and squeeze gently. Let dry.

6 Coat twice with matt varnish, allowing it to dry between coats, and then let dry completely.

7 Now is the time to decide if you want all petals going in the same direction on each earring or as a mirror image. Glue the findings onto the back of the earring. Make sure you position them off-center so the earrings won't be too close and rub against your cheek. Strengthen the back of the daisy with a small circle of colored cardstock before gluing the findings on if necessary, but make sure it is not visible through the holes.

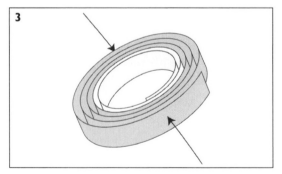

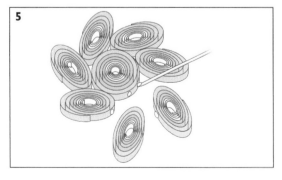

MILLEFIORI BUTTERFLY BROOCH

My mother used to have a tiny millefiori glass paperweight and the hundreds of tiny colored circles in it fascinated me. I've adapted the idea to make this fabulous, glossy butterfly brooch.

YOU WILL NEED

Pencil and paper

⅛in (3mm) wide scraps of different-colored quilling paper

Quilling tool or toothpick

White (PVA) glue

Sharp, pointed scissors

Colored cardstock

Craft knife and cutting mat

Toothpick

Découpage gloss varnish and paintbrush

Scraps of thin wire

Round-nose jewelry pliers

Brooch finding

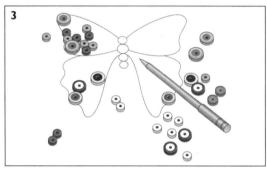

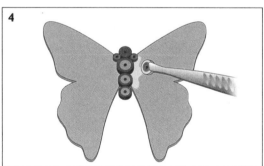

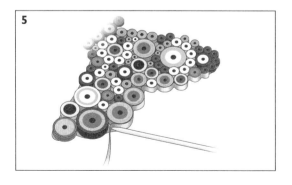

I Draw a butterfly shape on a piece of paper (or see template on page 123).

2 Make lots of closed coils of all different sizes and color combinations (see pages 71–72), but make sure there are two of every motif so you can make your butterfly wings a mirror image of each other. Choose a simple color combination for the body and make four closed coils for it.

3 Start to fill up the butterfly shape with the coils, matching the left wing to the right. Bring the coils right out to the sides so they come over the edges a little. Carry on until the butterfly is complete. Make some smaller coils in case you need a few extra.

4 Cut a butterfly shape out of colored cardstock and score lightly around the body from top to bottom on the underneath of the card. Gently fold the wings upward a little. Begin by putting some white (PVA) glue onto the cardstock body and glue on the body coils. Put a dab of glue on the sides of the coils where they touch each other.

5 Transfer all the coils from the paper shape onto the cardstock shape, a few at a time. Put white (PVA) glue on the cardstock first and, as you attach each coil, put a dab of glue on any side that will touch another coil. You may need to alter the design a little. Dab white (PVA) glue around the edge of the butterfly and wrap paper strips around the shape to prevent any coils from falling off. Ease it around the shapes with a toothpick.

7 Pull the wings up a little and balance them on lids, pushing the body down gently. Then varnish several times with découpage gloss varnish and let dry.

8 Make two antennae out of thin wire. Take the end of a wire in a pair of round-nose jewelry pliers and twist it once around the tips of the pliers. Glue the antennae to the underneath of the brooch. Attach the brooch finding.

TIARA

This fun accessory is suitable for any age. Try it in candy pink and powder blue for a little girl or make this more sophisticated version in gold and hot pink. Cover the headband with ribbon if you can't find one in the right color.

YOU WILL NEED

Paper

Gold quilling paper: ⅜in, ¼in, ⅛in (10mm, 5mm, 3mm)

Pink quilling paper: ⅛in (3mm)

Quilling tool or toothpick

White (PVA) glue

Needle and thread

Pink, fabric-covered headband

Pitcher (jug)

Fixative or hairspray (oil and lanolin free)

Flat-backed pink diamantés

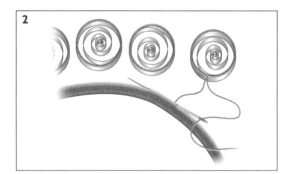

2

3a

3b

1 Make up all the closed and open coils (see page 73) and arrange them into position on a piece of paper (see diagram on page 124). I used a circle guide to make my coils the same size but you could make them by eye.

Gold coils
6 open—⅜in (10mm) wide; half a paper strip;
¾in (20mm) diameter circle
7 open—¼in (5mm) wide; half a paper strip; ⅝in (15mm) diameter circle (pinch four of these to make teardrops—see page 73)
2 closed—⅛in (3mm) wide; one paper strip
4 closed—⅛in (3mm) wide; half a paper strip
Pink coils
8 open—⅛in (3mm) wide; quarter of a paper strip;
⅜in (10mm) diameter circle
3 open—⅛in (3mm) wide; half a paper strip; ⅝in (15mm) diameter circle (pinch these to make teardrops—see page 73)

2 Ensure the end of the coil is on the bottom and sew through the outer layer of the coil onto the headband. Sew on the base coils one at a time. Turn the tiara over and go back along the coils, sewing them on from the back as well if they need to be stabilized a bit more.

3 Balance the tiara upright on something like a pitcher (jug) and begin to glue all the other coils onto the base coils, putting a dab of glue everywhere a coil touches another coil. The coils are not the same width so center them on each other.

4 Let dry. Spray with fixative or hairspray, and glue a few pink diamantés onto the closed coils to add a bit of sparkle.

SNOWFLAKES AND SPIDERS

Festive jewelry is always fun and brings a smile to your face. These designs are so versatile—you can make them in any color to fit any occasion. These delicate shapes can be made into earrings or simply add a piece of cord or very fine ribbon to make a choker. Diagrams for the shapes are on page 125.

The blue snowflake is made from quarter quills all the same size, ⅜in (10mm), to show you can make an intricate pattern from very simple shapes of circles and teardrops.

The sliver-blue and white snowflake is composed of several different shapes and sizes. Sometimes it helps to plan a complex shape out first on some paper that you've drawn a few guidelines on.

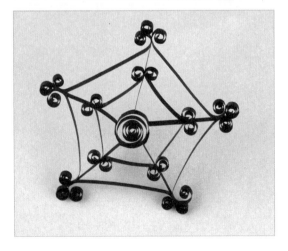

String a spider's web onto a thin piece of black cord to make a Halloween necklace. The spider's web has a central open coil with five spokes attached. Add scrolls in graduating sizes, and finish off by turning the ends of the spokes into open coils.

The white snowflake is made from simple ⅜in (10mm) quilled shapes too, with scrolls added (see page 73).

CHAINMAIL EARRINGS

Pearlized quilling strips come in wonderful metallic finishes and I was immediately reminded of chainmail armor, so I experimented until I found an easy way to make and link loops together. They give the effect of metal but without the weight.

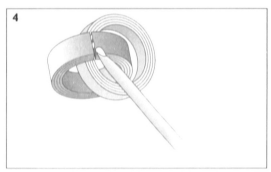

YOU WILL NEED

⅛in (3mm) wide strips of quilling paper in pearlized gray, silver, and fawn

Knitting needle or tube, ⅜in (10mm) diameter

Quilling tool or toothpick

White (PVA) glue

Satin varnish and paintbrush

Shallow saucer (optional)

Craft knife and cutting mat

Toothpicks

Earring findings

1 Using the gray, silver, and fawn quilling paper, make 38 closed coils with a wide central hole using the knitting needle or tube (see page 72).

2 Varnish the coils twice with satin varnish, not only to give them a nice sheen, but also to strengthen them as you will cut some of them. You can place the coils in a shallow saucer to make it easier to coat them all over. Let dry on the end of a toothpick.

3 Arrange the coils in position (see diagram on page 124). Check the earring findings. You may need to cut some paper strips in half lengthwise to make thinner circles to fit through the finding's loop.

4 Start from the top coil and cut through the circle immediately below it. Place the circle so that it is standing up on your cutting mat and make a cut on the bottom of the circle with a sharp craft knife. Slide the first circle and the third circle onto the second circle and glue the cut back together again. Let dry. You now have the beginning of a chain.

5 Work through all the other coils, making as few cuts as possible, and join them up into chains.

6 Attach the findings to the chains.

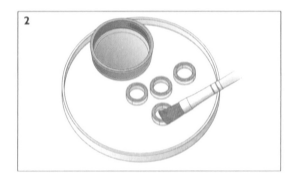

2

4

SUMMER BASKET NECKLACE

Bright, bold, and colorful, this project is perfect for summer's intense colors. It would also be fantastic if made in pearlized colors to go with the chainmail earrings.

YOU WILL NEED

⅛in (3mm) wide strips of quilling paper in a selection of yellow and orange

Tubes of various diameters: ⅜in, ¾in, 1⅛in (10mm, 20mm, 30mm)

Quilling tool or toothpick

White (PVA) glue

Matt varnish and paintbrush

Saucer (optional)

Craft knife and cutting mat

Toothpicks

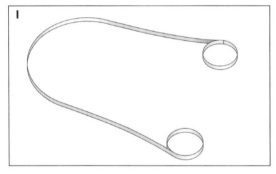

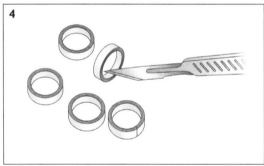

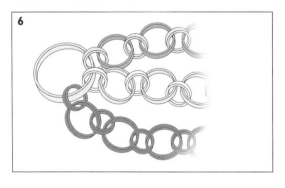

1 Use a spare paper strip and make a coil at either end to help you decide how far down you want the basket strands to start. I made two open coils of 1⅛in (30mm) diameter for the ends of the neck chain. Use the paper strip as a guide to find how many coils you will need in total for the neck chain. I used 45 ⅜in (10mm) closed coils with a wide central hole using the smallest tube in two alternating colors for the neck chain (see page 72). Bear in mind you will need to put this over your head without damaging it.

2 Make enough coils for three strands of ¾in (20mm) coils alternating with and starting and ending with ⅜in (10mm) links. One has nine ¾in (20mm) coils with 10 links; one has ten ¾in (20mm) coils with 11 links; and one has eleven ¾in (20mm) coils with 12 links. Choose your own color arrangements.

3 Varnish all the coils and links twice with matt varnish to strengthen them as you will cut some of them. You can place them in a shallow saucer to make it easier to coat them all over. Let dry on the end of a toothpick.

4 Arrange the coils into the three strands. Cut through the links by standing them upright on a cutting mat and using a craft knife to slice through the bottom. Slide the larger coils onto the links and glue the links back together with a small dab of glue.

5 Work through all the coils in the neck chain by cutting alternate links and making them into a chain as before.

6 Attach one end of all the strands to one of the large coils first. Then attach the other ends of the strands to the other large link, and finally, attach the neck chain. Make sure you have glued all the links closed.

* * * * * * * * * * * * * * * *

CHAPTER FOUR

FOLDING

TECHNIQUES AND EQUIPMENT

Some of the projects in this chapter use geometric shapes. It's very important that these are cut out as accurately as possible. Generally, I don't advocate using much special equipment; that decision is up to you. However, I am prepared to spend money on shape punches, especially circle punches, as without them the projects wouldn't work as well. If you cut your circles by hand and have to glue layers together, you may be disappointed by the results as the edges may not match up.

PAPERS

It is important that you choose the right paper for the right technique. For example, you may have fallen in love with a heavily embossed gift wrap paper. Before you buy sheets of it, experiment with one first. You may find the embossing cracks if you try to fold it or it may flake off when you cut it with a blade. Then you will realize that it is probably only suitable for a little gentle manipulation and rolling. Maybe you have learnt your lesson on a thick paper and you buy some very thin paper. That comes with its own problems, too. It may not hold shapes very well and is so thin that you have to cut hundreds of circles, instead of tens, to make a pompom.

The pompom and bobble projects (see pages 98–103 and 104–5) are best made with paper that has dye throughout so you don't get a white edge when you cut the paper. Otherwise, the color effect is lost when the circles are made into spheres as the white edges will show the most.

Some of these projects are perfect for using up old bits of paper you've been saving. I used the insides of envelopes, magazine pages, and plain white paper for some of mine.

PUNCHES

Which ones to choose? There are so many out there. My advice is to buy a simple one first and see how you get on with using it. It's wonderful being able to cut several shapes in one go and really speeds things up. Sometimes I punch shapes out of tissue paper and candy wrappers. The punch is not always happy when I try this and the motifs get screwed up. I find I get the best result if I sandwich the offending papers between two thin layers of standard white paper.

If you do cut shapes by hand, be careful to cut them as accurately as possible. Do not swap between different units of measurement when making the projects, because the conversions are not exact.

ADDING COLOR

Generally, I don't paint my projects. Instead, I usually use paper that's already colored or has an interesting pattern.

FOLDING

It helps if, when you have to make a fold, you use your fingernail or a folding tool to smooth the crease down. Some people use a paper folder which is used a lot in origami.

FIXING

I try to use a varnish on my projects whenever possible. Some of the projects in this chapter don't lend themselves to being varnished. Try to varnish a spare piece first to see how it affects the color and movement, but be careful not to drench the paper. If I can't use varnish, I try a burst of fixative or even an inexpensive hairspray. It has to be one without lanolin or oils and the cheaper ones tend to leave those out.

EQUIPMENT

Set square
Cutting mat
Craft knife
Ruler
Sharp, pointed scissors
Paper folder
Punches
Paper clips (useful for holding papers together)
Pins
Tweezers
Toothpicks
Small, thin tubes
Varnish, fixative, or hairspray

ZIGZAG NECKLACE

Use contrasting colored paper to show off your zigzags to their best advantage. I only tied soft knots in this version but I have made others with several knots and they look just as stunning.

YOU WILL NEED

¼in (5mm) wide strips of quilling paper: 10 mustard yellow, 6 dark brown, 4 sage green

Masking tape

White (PVA) glue

Matt varnish and paintbrush (optional)

Fixative or hairspray (oil and lanolin free)

Small hole punch or needle

Hemp thread: dark maroon, mustard yellow

Sharp, pointed scissors

1 Make six zigzags from mustard yellow and dark brown and six zigzags from mustard yellow and sage green.

2 Start a zigzag by placing one strip vertically on your work table. Place the other color strip horizontally and at a right angle on top of it, leaving ⅜in (10mm) of each strip before the intersection. Anchor the strips by putting some masking tape onto the ⅜in (10mm) tails. Keeping the horizontal strip flat on the table, bend the perpendicular strip upward, and fold it back neatly around the horizontal strip. Press along the fold.

3 Keeping the vertical strip flat, fold the horizontal strip to the left, back onto itself. Bring the vertical strip back down over the horizontal one again and carry on alternating the strips, using your nail to sharpen up the creases. Continue until you nearly run out of paper.

4 Join together six mustard yellow and six dark brown zigzags. Trim the end of each zigzag so it is square, overlap it into another zigzag, and glue into position. The zigzags change color depending on which direction they go in so you can decide what effect you want. Join the remaining four mustard yellow and four sage green zigzags together.

5 These can be awkward to varnish, so try some matt varnish on a spare piece of paper first (see page 92). If you have problems, use hairspray or an artist's fixative spray to give it a little protection. Let dry.

6 Weave the longer, yellow/brown, strand around the yellow/sage one and tie a loose knot (see photo, left). Finish off the ends by making a small hole in the end of each strand with a small hole punch or needle.

7 Tie a knot in one end of each piece of hemp and thread them through the holes in the zigzags. Allow enough hemp thread to put the necklace on over your head. Thread the ends through the holes at the other end of the zigzags. Finish with a knot and trim the thread.

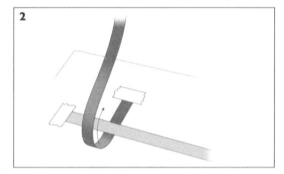

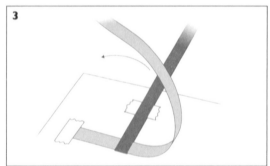

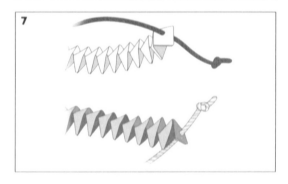

ZIGZAG EARRINGS

Accuracy is essential when making these. Practice on some wide paper strips first until you have mastered the technique. I made each of my earrings in different colorways to match a necklace, but you could do each of them exactly the same.

YOU WILL NEED

⅛in (3mm) wide strips of quilling paper: two mustard yellow, one dark brown, one sage green

Masking tape

Sharp, pointed scissors

White (PVA) glue

Fixative or hairspray (oil and lanolin free)

Matt varnish and paintbrush (optional)

Needle

Earring findings

1 Make one zigzag from mustard yellow and dark brown and one zigzag from mustard yellow and sage green.

2 Start a zigzag by placing one strip vertically on your work table. Place the other color strip horizontally and at a right angle on top of it leaving ⅜in (10mm) of each strip before the intersection. Anchor the strips by putting some masking tape onto the ⅜in (10mm) tails.

3 Keeping the horizontal strip flat on the table with your right hand, bend the perpendicular strip upward with your left hand, and fold it back neatly and tightly onto itself around the horizontal strip. Press along the fold with your fingernail.

4 Now keeping the vertical strip flat and immovable, fold the horizontal strip to the left, back onto itself. Bring the vertical strip back down over the horizontal one again and carry on alternating the strips, using your nail to sharpen up the creases as you go. After you have got the zigzag going, you can pick it up and do it in your hands. You must try to keep the folds as square and on top of one another as you can. Continue until you nearly run out of paper.

5 Tie a couple of knots in each strand and, when you are happy with the results, trim the ends so they are square, overlap them a little, and join them up with some glue.

6 These can be awkward to varnish and some papers may be too absorbent. Try some matt varnish on a spare piece of paper first. Be careful not to drench the paper. When it has dried, the strands are more rigid and don't move so fluidly. If you have problems, use an inexpensive hairspray or an artist's fixative spray to give it a little protection. Let dry.

7 Make a small hole in each strand with a needle, and then attach findings.

RA-RA POMPOM NECKLACE

This is an advanced project so it may be better to start with something simpler to begin with. Try out the Pompom Ring (pages 102–3) first to see how you get on. Alternatively, just make the pompoms and thread them onto a spare chain necklace. It only takes practice to be accurate.

YOU WILL NEED

Double-sided colored paper (approx. 110gsm) in stone, purple, blue, yellow

Circle punch, 1½in (38mm) diameter

Thin tube, approx. ¼in (5mm) diameter

White (PVA) glue

Toothpicks

White cardstock

Pencil

Pincushion and pins

Needles and thread

Fixative or hairspray (oil and lanolin free)

String

Sharp, pointed scissors

Beading thread

Matt varnish and paintbrush

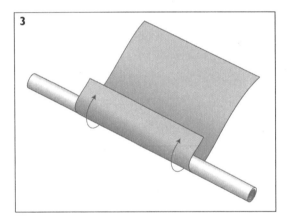

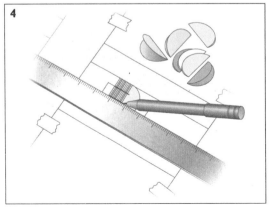

1 Make three pompoms by punching 162 circles. Each pompom has 54 circles. I used 30 stone, 8 purple, 8 blue, and 8 yellow for each pompom and I scattered the colored circles randomly.

2 To make one pompom, fold 54 circles in half and run your fingernail or a folding tool along each crease to define it more. Arrange them in a pile with the color order you want.

3 Make a center tube for the pompom by rolling a 2 x 2⅜in (50 x 60mm) blue paper rectangle around the tube and gluing it.

4 Place two strips of white cardstock 1½in (38mm) apart. Arrange an overlapping row of the half circles (try just a few to begin with) between them and mark them into thirds with a pencil, just along their folds. You can place some paper that is already marked at right angles to the card to help divide them into thirds.

5 Take the shapes, a few at a time, and pierce two holes in each with a pin, close to the folded edge. Use the pencil marks as a guide so the holes will line up. Placing the shapes on a pincushion when you make the holes will help.

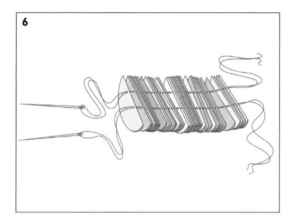

6 Thread the shapes onto two needles using doubled thread, pull them close together but leave several inches of thread free at both ends. Stand them with the folds up.

7 Coat the middle of the tube with glue, center it vertically along the middle of the folds, and pull the threads gently so the pompom tightens around the tube. Knot the threads and trim the ends. Put a dab of glue on them. Nudge the half circles gently into place. Let dry.

8 Put some glue around the edge of each pompom. Let dry. Note that it's impossible to varnish these so I spray them with fixative or inexpensive hairspray that contains no oil or lanolin. Repeat for the other two pompoms.

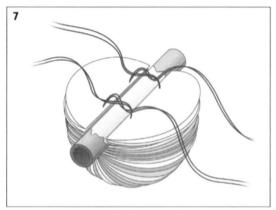

9 Measure how long you want your necklace to be so you can pull it on over your head. Make a circle from a piece of string and use it as a guide for where you want to position your pompoms. I placed mine off-center.

10 Make thin tubes by rolling 2 x ¾in (50 x 20mm) paper rectangles around toothpicks and gluing. Varnish twice with matt varnish and let dry. Arrange them in position around your string guide and between the pompoms. Cut some tubes in half so that the necklace will sit better around the neck.

11 Cut three lengths of beading thread the same length as your necklace and leave extra length for tying. Start halfway down one side and start to thread your tube beads in threes on separate theads. Gently tie a knot before and after each trio so the tubes fit snugly together. Be careful not to pull the thread so tightly that it cuts into the beads. Thread on the pompoms when you come to them.

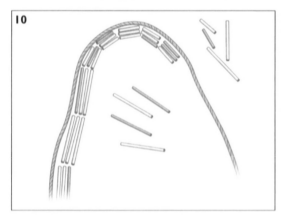

12 Tie a knot to finish, put a dab of glue on the knot, and hide the tails in the bead tubes.

RA-RA POMPOM RING

I love rings and this is a whopper. I'd advise wearing it on your middle finger so there is less danger of it being knocked and damaged.

YOU WILL NEED

Double-sided colored paper (approx. 110gsm) in stone, purple, blue, yellow

Circle punch, 1½in (38mm) diameter

Pincushion and pins

Needle and thread

Toothpicks

White (PVA) glue

Fixative or hairspray (oil and lanolin free)

Tube that is the same diameter as your finger

Sharp, pointed scissors

Matt varnish and paintbrush

Blue cardstock

1 Make one pompom. Punch out 48 circles. I used 20 stone, 6 purple, 6 blue, and 6 yellow and I scattered the colors randomly.

2 Fold all the circles in half and run your fingernail or a folding tool along each crease to define it. Arrange them in a pile with the color order you want.

3 Take the shapes, a few at a time, and pierce a central hole in each, close to the folded edge. Placing the shapes on a pincushion when you make the holes will help.

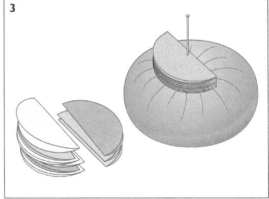

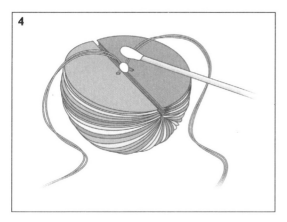

4 Thread the shapes onto a needle using doubled thread, pull them close together but leave several inches of thread free at both ends. Stand them with the folds up. Pull the threads gently so the pompom tightens until it makes a half sphere. Knot the threads and trim. Put a dab of glue on them. Nudge the half circles gently into place. It's impossible to varnish this so I spray it with fixative or inexpensive hairspray that contains no oil or lanolin.

5 Cut a long strip of paper 9½ x ⅝in (240 x 15mm) and roll up around a tube that is the size of your finger, putting some glue on it as you roll it up. Varnish twice with matt varnish and let dry.

6 Punch two circles out of blue cardstock. Glue the pompom onto one circle and ease the half circles into a good position. Put some glue around the ends of the pompom.

7 Stitch the remaining blue cardstock circle onto the ring when it is dry. Decide which direction you want your pompom to face and place the circle slightly off-center if you need to make it fit your finger shape better. Glue it onto the cardstock circle underneath the pompom.

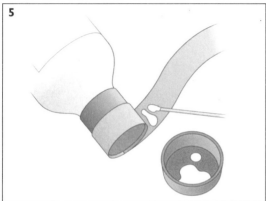

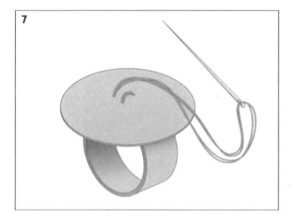

BOBBLE EARRINGS

You need a circular hole punch to make these and once you have punched all your circles, you can arrange them into different patterns. And it's so satisfying to use up a broken chain. They would look really interesting if you made small bobbles as well as large ones.

YOU WILL NEED

Double-sided colored pearlized paper (approx. 120gsm) in pink and blue

Circle punch, ⅝in (15mm) diameter

Glue stick or white (PVA) glue

10¼in (260mm) thin chain

Wire cutters

Earring findings

Fixative or hairspray (oil and lanolin free)

1 Punch 36 blue and 36 pink circles. Each bobble has nine blue and nine pink circles.

2 Fold all the circles in half and run your fingernail or a folding tool along each crease.

3 Make four half bobbles with a blue center. Take one blue half circle and glue a pink shape to the left and to the right of it. I found it easier to use a glue stick but you could use white (PVA) glue. Glue a blue shape to the left and the right of the pink ones. Then add another pink one to each side, and another blue one to finish off. From underneath, you should see two blue shapes, as in the top illustration.

4 Make four half bobbles with a pink center. Alternate two blue, two pink, two blue, and two pink shapes on either side of the central half circle. From underneath, you should see two pink shapes, as in the bottom illustration.

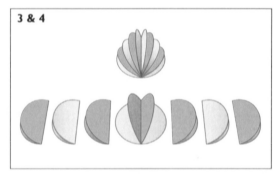

5 Cut the chain in half.

6 Make one earring. Glue two half bobbles, one with a pink center and one with a blue center, together and sandwich one end of the chain in the middle. Add another bobble to the other end of the chain. Assemble the other earring. Let the glue dry.

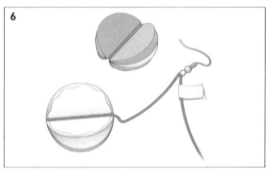

7 Slide the chains through the findings to the length you want. I did mine to 2in (50mm).

8 The earrings are impossible to varnish. The pearlized paper has a coating, which helps protect them a little. To protect the earrings further, spray with an inexpensive hairspray that is oil and lanolin free or an artist's fixative spray (after testing it on some spare paper first). Be careful not to drench the paper.

CABBAGE ROSE CORSAGE

I have made so many versions of this in different papers and every one has received compliments. And they are so simple to make. Finishing them with a large central bead makes them look more sophisticated.

YOU WILL NEED

White paper (approx. 120gsm)

Textured pink paper

Sharp, pointed scissors

Paintbrush and water

Thin tube or knitting needle

White (PVA) glue

Toothpick

Matt varnish and paintbrush (optional)

Fixative or hairspray (oil and lanolin free)

Pearl or papier mâché bead

Brooch finding

1 Using the template on page 126, cut three shapes from white paper.

2 Make three rough-edged shapes from the pink paper by drawing the template outline onto the paper with water and gently tearing it to give a soft edge.

3 Make the roses. Curl all the petals outward. With the right side of the paper uppermost, place the tip of each petal around a slim tube, and roll it away from you using your thumbs and forefingers. If you use a knitting needle, make sure it is not too long or it will be awkward to use.

4 With the right side of the papers uppermost, put a little glue around the central holes, and glue the pink shapes on top of the white ones.

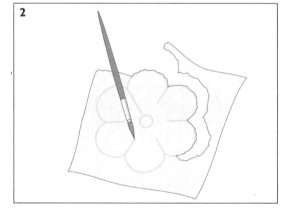

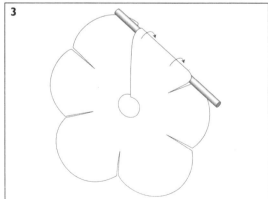

5 Form one shape into a wide cone. Pull the shape open a little at the split, and put some glue on the bottom third of the back of the paper. Pull it inside to overlap by one and a half petals to form a cone. Hold it firmly for a moment for the glue to set.

6 Form the second shape into a tighter cone by overlapping two and a half petals. Finally, make the third cone as tight as you can by continuing to pull the center petal to overlap all the petals.

7 Assemble the cones without gluing first so you can choose the best arrangement for the petals. Then put some glue around the bottom third of the tightest cone and insert it into the next tightest cone. Repeat the procedure into the largest cone. Push down into place firmly with a pencil. Trim petals if necessary to neaten.

8 The flowers can be awkward to varnish and some papers may be too absorbent. Try some matt varnish on a spare piece of paper first. Be careful not to drench the paper. If you have problems, use an inexpensive hairspray that is oil and lanolin free or an artist's fixative spray to give it a little protection. Let dry.

9 Cut the bottom of the rose a little flatter, glue in a pearl or papier mâché bead to finish off the center, and attach it to a brooch finding.

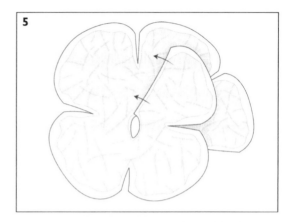

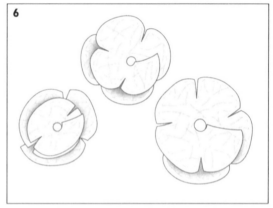

BROCADE HEADBAND

I wanted these pretty little flowers to look like fabric and I found a paper with a brocade pattern, which gives just the right effect. The paper sheets weren't big but you only need a small amount. You could easily adapt it and cover the whole of the headband for a bridesmaid.

YOU WILL NEED

Brocade or patterned paper (approx. 120gsm)

Sharp, pointed scissors

Thin tube or knitting needle

White (PVA) glue

Toothpick

Pencil

Matt varnish and paintbrush (optional)

Fixative or hairspray (oil and lanolin free)

Pearl or papier mâché beads

Narrow, fabric-covered headband

Needle and thread

1 Cut nine paper shapes in total using the template on page 126. Each rose will need three paper shapes.

2 Make a rose. Curl all the petals outward. With the right side of the paper uppermost, place the tip of each petal around a slim tube, and roll it away from you using your thumbs and forefingers. If you use a knitting needle, make sure it is not too long or it will be too awkward to use.

3 Form one shape into a wide cone. Pull the shape open a little at the split and put some glue on the bottom third of the back of the paper. Pull it inside to overlap by one and a half petals to form a cone. Hold it firmly for a moment for the glue to set.

4 Form the second shape into a tighter cone by overlapping two and a half petals. Finally, make the third cone as tight as you can by continuing to pull the center petal to overlap all the petals.

6 Assemble the cones without gluing first so you can choose the best arrangement for the petals. Then put some glue around the bottom third of the tightest cone and insert it into the next tightest cone. Repeat the procedure into the largest cone. Push down into place firmly with a pencil. Trim petals if necessary to neaten.

7 These can be awkward to varnish and some papers may be too absorbent. Try some matt varnish on a spare piece of paper first. Be careful not to drench the paper. If you have problems, use an inexpensive cheap hairspray that is oil and lanolin free or an artist's fixative spray to give it a little protection. Let dry.

8 Sew onto a fabric headband, using a pearl or papier mâché bead in the middle of each rose.

ROSE CORSAGES

All of these roses are made with the same template, but it's amazing how different they can look, just by using different types of paper. The paper you use should be firm enough to hold the petals' curls, but not so stiff that it cracks when you shape it.

Some kinds of papers will sadly be too thick, so try rolling a small scrap of the paper you want to use around a pencil first to test how well it curls. If you want to use a delicate tissue paper, you can double it up with a more substantial paper to help define the shape.

The blue version is made from the inside of old envelopes. I chose three that were of a similar blue but that had distinctive and different patterns and then glued a molded rose bead into the middle.

The flowered one is recycled from paper from a present someone had wrapped for me. I loved the paper and kept it. I painted a papier mâché pulp bead with a muted pink for the center.

The subtle green flower is made from some glossy magazine fashion pages. The model stood in front of a lovely, moody background of trees and stones. I made sure I didn't have any of the model on the templates when I cut them out. I decided to make a few stamens out of some spare beads I had to add a touch of sparkle as a contrast.

POSY CHOKER

Don't waste a drop of your old nail polish and use it instead of varnish on these vivid blossoms. Cluster a few together and suspend them with delicate ribbon or thread from an old necklace that you haven't worn for a while.

YOU WILL NEED

White paper (approx. 120gsm)

Sharp, pointed scissors

Toothpicks

White (PVA) glue

Nail polish in various colors

8 seed beads

Metal choker or other necklace

Beading thread and needle

Thin, gold satin ribbon

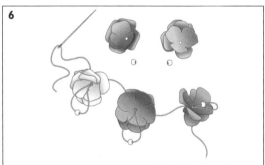

1 Cut 16 paper shapes in total using the template on page 126. Each flower will need two paper shapes.

2 Make a flower. Curl all the petals outward. With the right side of the paper uppermost, place the tip of each petal around a toothpick and roll it away from you using your thumbs and forefingers.

3 Form one shape into a wide cone. Pull the shape open a little at the split, and put some glue on the bottom third of the back of the paper. Pull it inside to overlap by one and a half petals to form a cone. Hold it firmly for a moment for the glue to set. Form the second shape into a tighter cone by overlapping three and a half petals.

4 Assemble the cones without gluing first so you can choose the best arrangement for the petals. Then put some glue around the bottom third of the tightest cone and insert it into the other cone. Make seven more flowers.

5 Coat the flowers, front and back, with nail polish. Use thin coats and do more than one if necessary.

6 Make a posy of five flowers. Arrange five flowers in a circle with a bead next to each. Make sure the beads are a little larger than the holes in the flowers. Leave a tail of 2¾in (7cm) and thread up from the bottom of the first flower, pick up its bead, and take the thread back down through the central hole. Move onto the next flower and repeat for the remaining three flowers.

7 Use a couple of stitches and sew one end of the ribbon close to the fifth flower. Pull the threads gently to draw the flowers together into a ball and the ribbon end will hide in the middle. Tweak the flowers into a good shape and tie a firm knot to hold them in place. Put a small dab of glue on the knot and trim the threads.

8 Make a three flower posy in the same way at the other end of the ribbon. Fold the ribbon where you want the lengths to be and make a loop over your choker and pull the two posies through.

VARIATION OF POSY CHOKER
MINI ROSE EARRINGS

Revitalize an old pair of stud earrings by pushing them through these miniature roses. You could even paint the roses the same color as your nails.

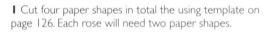

YOU WILL NEED

White paper (approx. 120gsm)

Sharp, pointed scissors

Toothpicks

White (PVA) glue

Nail polish

Small stud earrings

1 Cut four paper shapes in total the using template on page 126. Each rose will need two paper shapes.

2 Make a rose. Curl all the petals outward. With the right side of the paper uppermost, place the tip of each petal around a toothpick and roll it away from you using your thumbs and forefingers.

3 Form one shape into a wide cone. Pull the shape open a little at the split and put some glue on the bottom third of the back of the paper. Pull it inside to overlap by one and a half petals to form a cone. Hold it firmly for a moment for the glue to set.

4 Form the second shape into a tighter cone by overlapping three and a half petals.

5 Assemble the cones without gluing first so you can choose the best arrangement for the petals. Then put some glue around the bottom third of the tightest cone and insert it into the other cone.

6 Coat the roses, front and back, with nail polish. Use thin coats and do more than one if necessary. Let dry.

7 Recycle an old pair of stud earrings by pushing them through the middle of the flowers. You can trim the back of the rose down if it needs it.

TEMPLATES AND DIAGRAMS

WATERFALL BRACELET
DIAGRAM (pages 28–30)

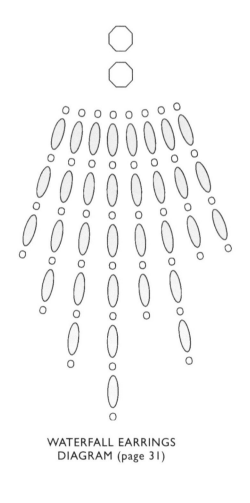

WATERFALL EARRINGS
DIAGRAM (page 31)

ICICLE EARRINGS TEMPLATE
(pages 32–33)

ICICLE EARRINGS
DIAGRAM (page 32–33)

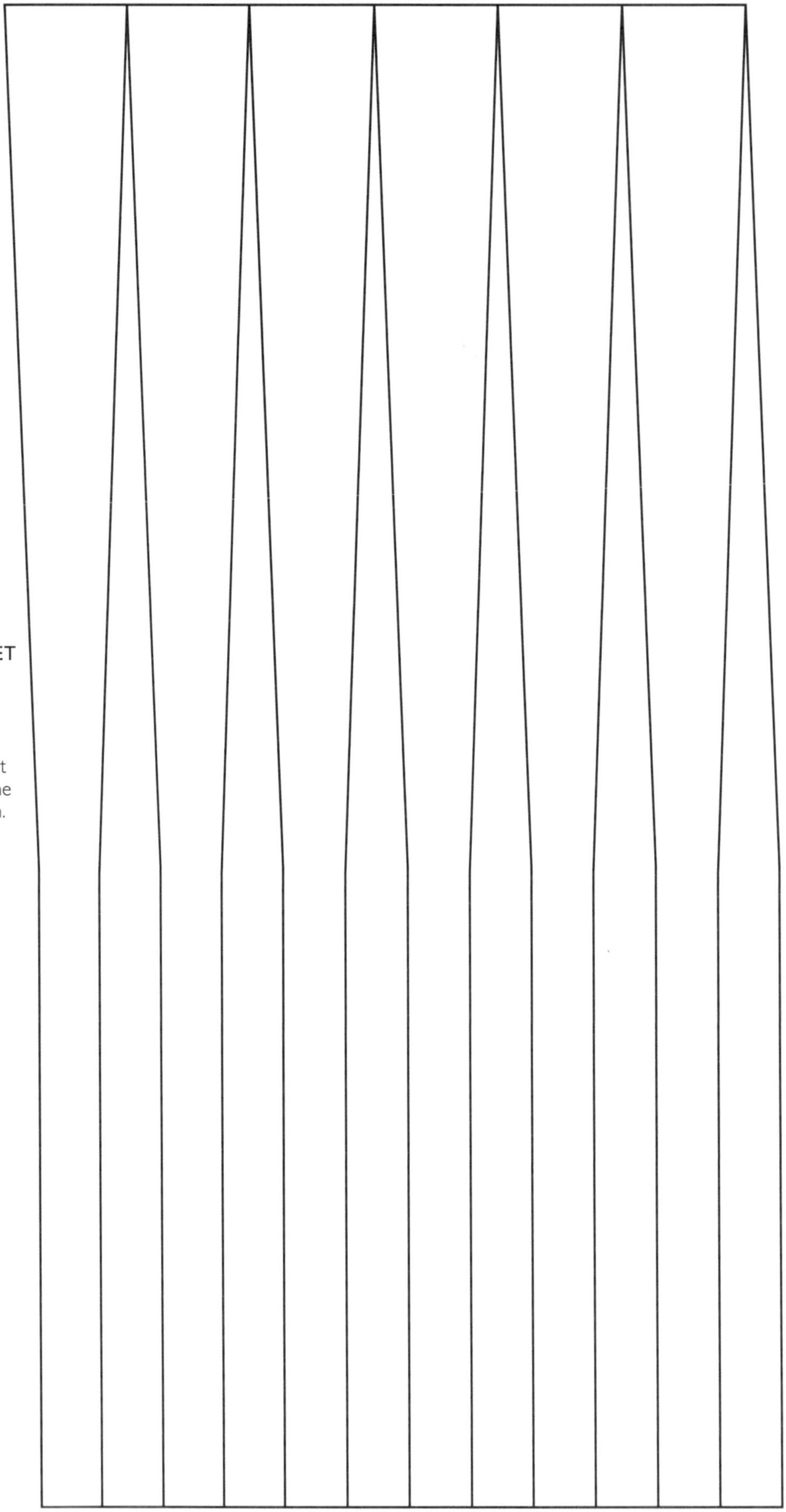

CHINA BRACELET
TEMPLATE
(pages 34–35)

Please note that
these are not exact
triangles—follow the
template as shown.

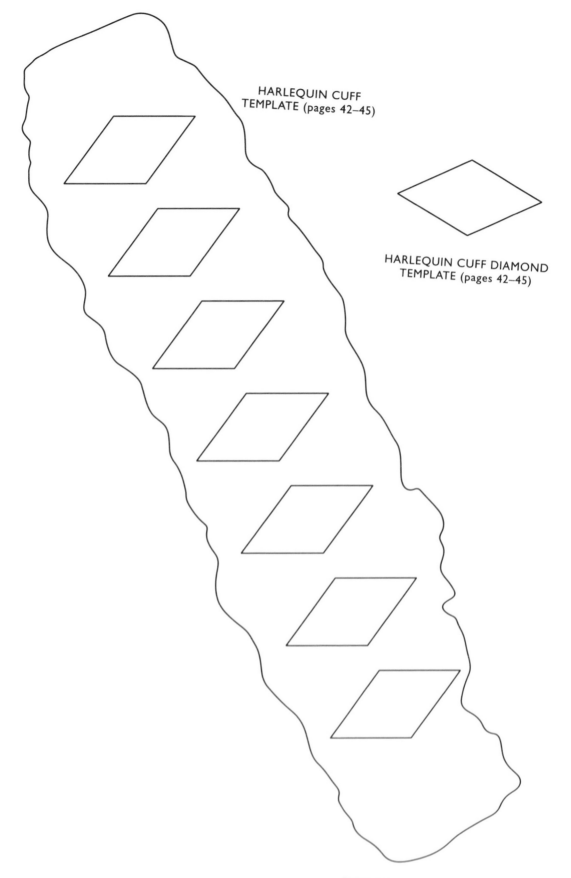

HARLEQUIN CUFF
TEMPLATE (pages 42–45)

HARLEQUIN CUFF DIAMOND
TEMPLATE (pages 42–45)

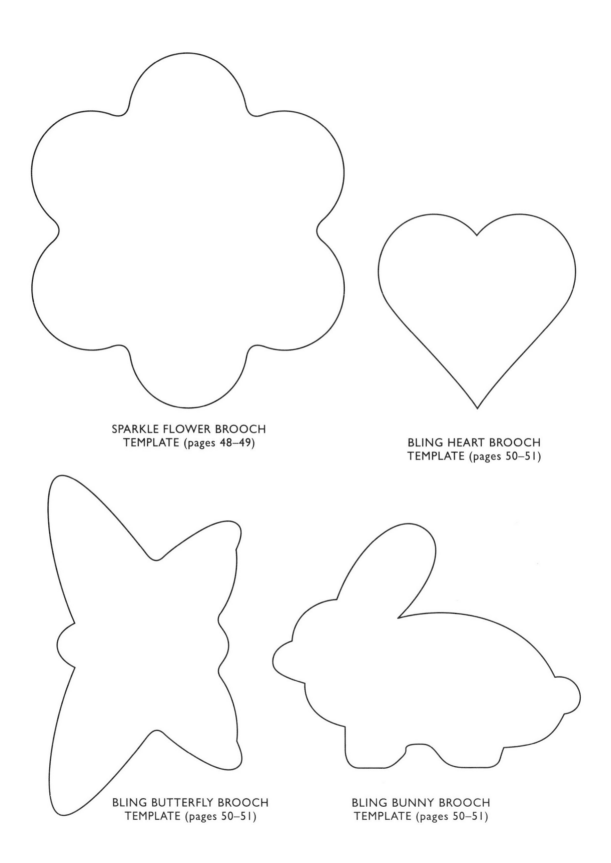

SPARKLE FLOWER BROOCH
TEMPLATE (pages 48–49)

BLING HEART BROOCH
TEMPLATE (pages 50–51)

BLING BUTTERFLY BROOCH
TEMPLATE (pages 50–51)

BLING BUNNY BROOCH
TEMPLATE (pages 50–51)

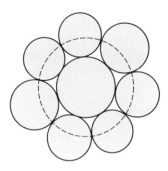

POP ART RING DIAGRAM
(pages 74–75)

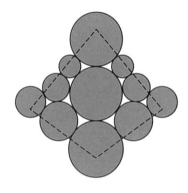

DIAMOND RING DIAGRAM
(pages 76–77)

MILLEFIORI BUTTERFLY BROOCH
TEMPLATE (pages 80–81)

GREEN DAISY EARRINGS
DIAGRAM (pages 78–79)

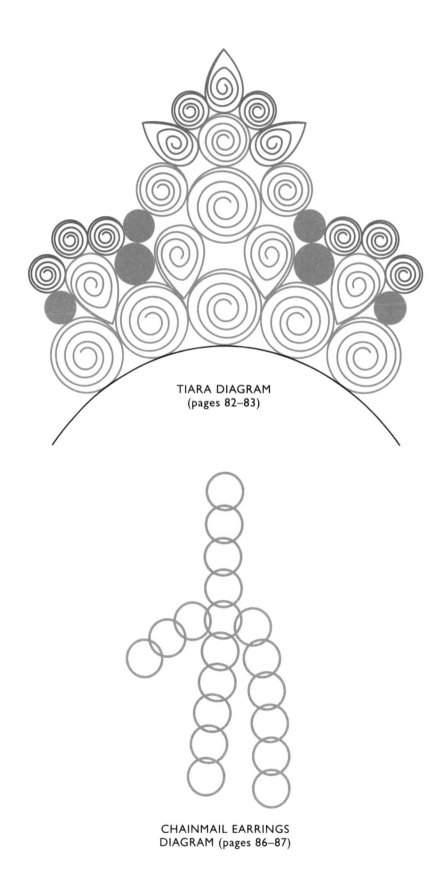

TIARA DIAGRAM
(pages 82–83)

CHAINMAIL EARRINGS
DIAGRAM (pages 86–87)

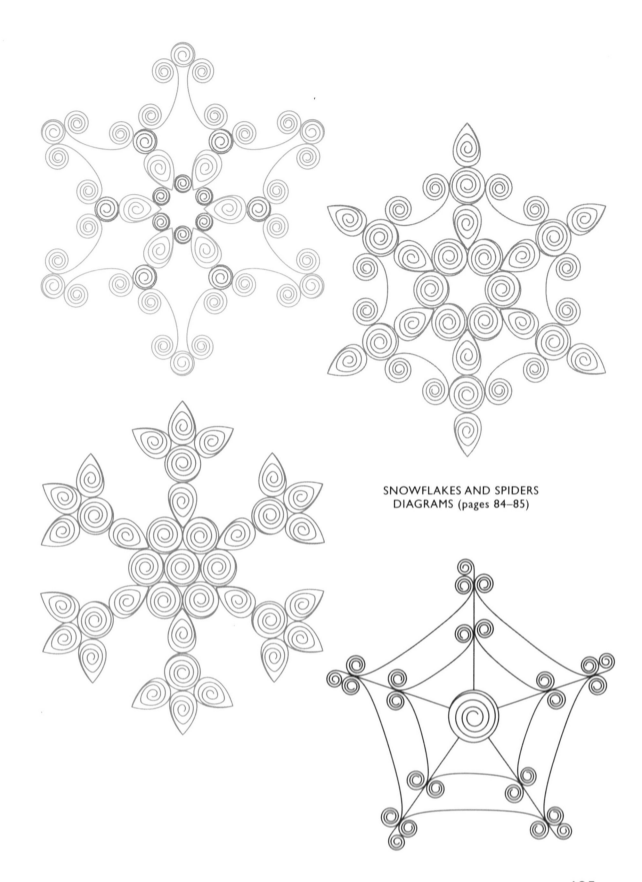

SNOWFLAKES AND SPIDERS
DIAGRAMS (pages 84–85)

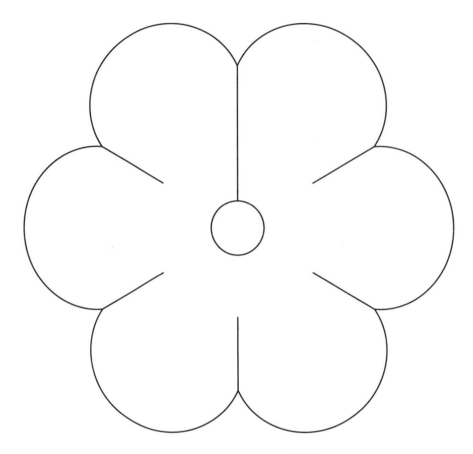

CABBAGE ROSE CORSAGE
TEMPLATE (pages 106–109)

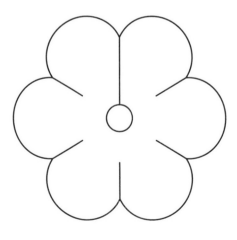

BROCADE HEADBAND ROSE
TEMPLATE (pages 110–111)

POSY CHOKER and MINI ROSE
EARRINGS TEMPLATE
(pages 114–115 and 116–117)

INDEX

SUPPLIERS

For paper and bead supplies, try the following websites.

US

A. C. Moore
www.acmoore.com

Fire Mountain Gems
www.firemountaingems.com

Hobby Lobby
www.hobbylobby.com

Jewelry Supply
www.jewelrysupply.com

Kate's Paperie
www.katespaperie.com

Lake City Craft Company
www.quilling.com

Michaels
www.michaels.com

Paper Source
www.paper-source.com

Quilled Creations
www.quilledcreations.com

UK

Beadworks
www.beadworks.co.uk

Beads Direct
www.beadsdirect.co.uk

Beads and Crystals
www.beadsandcrystals.co.uk

Elderberry Crafts
www.elderberrycrafts.com

Fred Aldous
www.fredaldous.co.uk

The Paper Trail
www.thepapertrail.org.uk

Hobbycraft
www.hobbycraft.co.uk

Paperchase
www.paperchase.co.uk

Shepherds Falkiners
www.falkiners.com

ACKNOWLEDGMENTS

Publishing a book involves the talents of many people and I would like to thank the team at CICO for all their hard work in putting this project together. Cindy Richards, the publisher, saw the potential in my idea and I am very grateful to her for including my book in her list. Also, I would like to thank my very supportive friends, Sally Powell in particular, who encouraged me to submit my idea in the first place and my partner, Jeff Marksz who was patience personified during the whole creative process.

A special mention is due to Peter Herring at Elderberry Crafts (www.elderberrycrafts.com) for his help and advice with quilling materials, and to Sue Woolnough at The Paper Trail (www.thepapertrail.org.uk).